# Be Your Own
# Executive Coach

# Be Your Own Executive Coach

## Master High-Impact Communications Skills for

➤ Dealing with difficult people
➤ Improving your personal image
➤ Learning how to listen
➤ Solving business problems creatively

## Peter deLisser

**Chandler House Press**
**Worcester, Massachusetts**

ISBN 1-886284-44-X
Library of Congress Catalog Card Number 98-89748
First Edition
ABCDEFGHIJK

**Published by**
Chandler House Press
335 Chandler Street
Worcester, MA 01602 USA

Chandler House Press books are available at special discounts for bulk purchases. For more information about how to arrange such purchases, please contact Chandler House Press, 335 Chandler Street, Worcester, MA 01602, or call (800) 642-6657, or fax (508) 756-9425, or find us on the World Wide Web at www.chandlerhousepress.com.

Chandler House Press books are distributed to the trade by
National Book Network
4720 Boston Way
Lanham, MD 20706
(800) 462-6420

# CONTENTS

# PREFACE

Question: Why should you read *Be Your Own Executive Coach?*
Answer: Your career, your family, and your life require it.

Those are strong words, but unless you gain an awareness and mastery of how you interact with others, you limit yourself and you cause problems for others.

Especially in the business world of today, there is constant pressure to do things faster, better, and with little room for error. This calls for managers, indeed everyone in an organization, to communicate clearly. Communication, after all, is what facilitates the smooth collaboration needed to get things done right the first time.

Peter Senge in his book, *The Fifth Discipline*, says, "a leader needs a communication system, which is what makes visible our limiting structures." *Be Your Own Executive Coach* helps you identify your limiting communication structures, and then, in jargon-free language, presents theory and practices that directly relate to business.

You'll discover the choices people make in every conversation. In essence, we can choose to communicate or to attack and defend. Unfortunately, people attack and defend most of the time because they have no understanding or system for doing otherwise. This book provides a system that will help you accept 100% responsibility for the quality of your conversations and communication—including those times when you're under great pressure.

**Question: When should you read this book?**

**Answer: Read this book when you're motivated to improve the quality of your communications on the job and in every difficult situation.**

It helps you hold up a mirror to see and hear what you sound like when interacting with others, particularly in pressure situations. Those are the situations where you especially don't want to make a mistake, where other people are affected, and that can reflect positively or negatively on your performance.

When you're motivated to improve, you'll read in a focused way, and then put into practice and apply this principle that serves as the foundation of this book: "I'm 100% responsible for the quality of each of my conversations because I

➤ consider each conversation an ethical process
➤ recognize my influence on the other person
➤ respect fully our spiritual and cultural differences."

**Question: What makes *Be Your Own Executive Coach* different?**

**Answer: Its impact on future generations.**

Every morning when I get up, I remind myself that my mission in life is to impact on future generations. I'll never forget when I came to that conclusion. An executive interrupted me in the middle of a communication workshop and said, "I'm damn mad at you." Startled I asked, "Why? What did I do to you?" His response was, "You're asking me to change three generations of communications—my father's, mine, and my son's."

Here are examples of how the on-the-job behavior of corporate leaders I've been privileged to coach has been affected by earlier generations.

➤ A Chinese executive is considered passive because he gives little feedback to his boss. He learned at home authority is to be respected and their requests carried out without question, particularly when in front of others.
➤ A Cuban executive has no hesitation confronting senior executives in staff meetings much to their dismay. He learned growing up in a tough neighborhood that you either spoke up or got put down.

➤ A Scandinavian executive finds it difficult to speak up in meetings dominated by sales and marketing executives who talk all the time. She was taught never to promote herself and believes that "self-praise stinks."

➤ A senior executive dominates young MBAs because he learned early in his life from his parents that nothing he does is good enough; he can always do better. Thus, there's no praise or acknowledgment for young executives who may try to impress him.

**Question: Who wrote *Be Your Own Executive Coach*?**
**Answer: Peter deLisser, a leadership coach.**

Peter deLisser has spent a lifetime coaching people to manage their careers. He started coaching 10th grade English students, then college football, wrestling, and baseball players at Williams College and Columbia University.

For the past 30 years he has coached business organizations to create cultures of responsible communication. His coaching takes place in four venues:

➤ In one-on-one leadership coaching of *Fortune* 100 high-potential and senior executives
➤ In team building for executives and their direct reports
➤ In conducting large strategic group workshops for sales and general managers
➤ By delivering keynote addresses at national meetings

His corporate clients include J.P. Morgan, Philip Morris, AT&T, Pfizer, Schering Plough, McGraw-Hill, Standard & Poor's, and Tetley U.S.A.

*Fortune* magazine acknowledged his current coaching by featuring him in their article "The Executive's New Coach." The International Listening Association, the American Institute of Certified Public Accountants, and the American Society of Training and Development have published his articles.

**Question: How should you approach reading this book?**
**Answer: It depends on your style of learning and what you're looking for.**

The four prevalent approaches are:

➤ Expect immediate results.
➤ Expect logical, orderly structure.
➤ Expect in-depth information presented in an interesting way.
➤ Expect ability to share content with others.

If you're a person who needs immediate results and not much theory, start with the 36 individual coaching stories. They're found in the shaded boxes throughout. Each relates how a specific executive solved a communication problem. Each story ends with an applicable communication principle. Start on page one and flip the pages continuously reading each story.

If you're a person who requires an orderly structure for information presented, start with Chapter 1, which presents an overview of the responsible communication process and then proceed logically chapter by chapter through the book.

If you're a person who values depth of information and understanding, start with any chapter you want! Each chapter stands alone. You may want to start with the chapters on "Responsible Listening" and "Responsible Speaking." Each ends with a variety of suggestions as to how to implement these two essential skills.

If you're a person who enjoys other people and likes consensus, show the table of contents to a couple of friends and ask them how they would approach reading the book. Most people find starting with Chapter 2 helpful. It highlights a variety of personal strategies to implement without needing to study and practice other related skills. It's easy to practice these with others.

Whatever you approach, by learning how to become your own executive coach, you'll find that people will listen to you better, understand you better, and become more productive—which means you'll be doing all these things as well!

## Why I Wrote this Book

I wrote this book for two reasons.

First I wanted to send a message to my five adult children and eight grandchildren that their ability to communicate is of equal importance with any technical skill they might acquire. Their careers, their relationships, and literally the quality of their lives depend on their communications.

The second reason I wrote this book is that I wanted business executives to know their ability to communicate is as important as any other skill they possess. I have had the opportunity to coach hundreds of highly motivated, talented executives whose careers might have been derailed if their companies had not had the good sense to invest in their *communications capital*. This book is their stories. It is what they taught me about the need for a disciplined system of personal communications. This is a system that they can put into practice, one that would change behaviors for the better, one that helps them work with others to achieve higher levels of performance, and one that assures them successful careers.

It will also send a message to their children and grandchildren—study communications: your life depends on it.

CHAPTER 1

# Master High-Impact Communications

*T*he value of high-impact communications comes from helping you in

➤ Dealing with difficult people
➤ Improving your personal image
➤ Learning how to listen
➤ Solving business problems creatively

I initially suggested to the publisher dramatic titles for this book, such as:

➤ *Master High-Impact Communications—A Life-Saving, Death-Defying Act*
➤ *Master High-Impact Communications—Your Career and Your Life Depend on It*

➤ *Master High-Impact Communications—Only the Courageous Survive*

I suggested those titles because I believe them.

If you are an executive committee member and the president owns all the stock and is passionately about to make a major blunder, it takes courage to risk your $500,000 salary to tell him he's wrong. Knowing how to communicate with difficult people is useful—to your career and pension.

If you're a hard-charging executive who intimidates other executives, who demean you when they refer to you as "dearie," it's worth a lot to improve your image. Reaching the goal of being a CEO is more important than continually trying to change a *southern* culture.

If you're the chairman of a company and intimidate all the newly hired, very expensive MBAs because you refuse to let them try to impress you with their limited knowledge, learning to listen—to prove you heard them, to consider their ideas at least briefly—will reduce the high cost of turnover.

If you're a project manager whose job is to solve problems with products and reposition them faster than competitors and you let your 160 I.Q. cause you to interrupt people before they get three words out of their mouths, then you tell them why their ideas are wrong and why yours is right, you will learn to be more creative by solving problems jointly.

These are real-life situations in which real people required life-saving, death-defying, courageous acts—or more appropriately—high-impact communication skills.

This book is about learning to coach yourself to use high-impact communication skills at the right time, in the right way.

## Master a Responsible Communications Process: The Four S's

When Senator Bill Bradley, the great New York Knicks basketball player, was asked what was the main reason for his success, he replied, "I always knew where I was on the court." Like Bill, leaders need to know at every moment where they are in a conversation if they expect to be their own executive coach. To be their own executive coach, they need to master high-impact communications, to communicate responsibly. (Responsible: Accountable, reliable, capacity for moral decisions—able to discharge obligations.)

Responsible Communications provide leaders with a process for knowing where they are and what they are doing ethically in every conversation, at every moment. The 4-S process focuses on:

➤ Strategies
➤ Structure
➤ Skills
➤ System

This process is essential to know and practice if we are to choose to:

➤ Be 100% responsible for the quality of our conversations
➤ Give up 100% trying to change others and work on changing our own habits
➤ Make 100% the choice to respect the religious and cultural differences of others

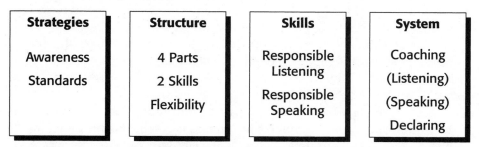

| Strategies | Structure | Skills | System |
|---|---|---|---|
| Awareness | 4 Parts | Responsible Listening | Coaching |
| Standards | 2 Skills | Responsible Speaking | (Listening) |
|  | Flexibility |  | (Speaking) |
|  |  |  | Declaring |

**Figure 1-1. Responsible Communications, the Four S's of communications**

Before we provide an overview of each of the Four S's, here's a coaching story. (You'll find such stories throughout the book. They all contain a principle of communications.)

This is a simple story about bacon and eggs, but it highlights the most important concept in all of the Responsible Communications Process—What is the objective of our conversations? Without a clear objective, each of our conversations has the potential for disaster.

---

### The Outcome of Our Conversations Depends on Our Objective

I walked into a self-service restaurant near Grand Central Station one morning and ordered fried eggs on whole wheat toast, with bacon. When it was ready, I took it to the table and sat down. If there's anything I love, it's hot bacon and eggs in the morning.

I cut the bacon, put a piece of it on top of the egg, took a bite, and said to myself, "The damn bacon is cold!"

I was furious! I love breakfast.

I started to walk up to the counter; I wanted to tell the man behind the counter that "the damn bacon is cold." By the time I reached the counter, my training in salesmanship had convinced me to change my objective. The objective was to get the bacon heated up, not to insult the man behind the counter. So I handed him the plate and said, "Please put the bacon on the grill. I'd like it hotter." (That was my new objective.)

He took it out of my hand and put it on the grill. I waited a few minutes. He handed it back. I said, "Thank you." He said, "You're welcome." I retreated to the table, to enjoy my breakfast.

The objective of a conversation is the most important part. It determines what the outcome will be. If my objective had been to insult the counterman, I'd have been successful, but I would have been angry and upset during the whole time I ate the bacon.

Having changed my objective, to having hot bacon, I respected the counterman and I enjoyed my breakfast. What a difference an objective can make! I love eating hot eggs and bacon—on a calm stomach.

---

Now let's get on to a brief overview of the 4-S process—Strategies, Structure, Skills, and System. Each will be thoroughly explained in separate chapters, which include theory, practical exercises, and coaching stories necessary for you to choose to be 100% responsible for the quality of your conversations.

## Personal Strategies Keep Our Careers on a Fast Track

In any business, game, or family, strategies are necessary to keep us on the straight path to reach our
goals. Although most of us spend 50% to 90% of our
time in interpersonal communications, we spend
almost no time studying and practicing it. We
assume that our communications are like breathing: they happen
naturally.

> **Strategies**
> Awareness
> Standards

Not true. They require personal strategies, strategies that
allow us to keep our careers on a fast track.

Why do we need strategies to keep our careers on a fast track?

One important reason is that we spend 10% of our time "communicating up." Senior managers see and hear us infrequently.
When they do, they tend to form lasting impressions. The careers
of senior and high-potential executives have been put on hold
because senior managers remember that once in a presentation
"she didn't answer questions directly" or that "he gave extreme
amounts of information." Since we have limited exposure to senior management, we need to practice and know how to communicate when the opportunity arises.

Another reason is that we spend 40% of our time with subordinates. The stories of how we treat them last a long time—"she
yells at her people" or "he micro manages them." Once these stories start to spread, they taint perceptions of our abilities to lead.

Because how we communicate and with whom impacts on our
careers, each of us must develop personal strategies in two areas:
awareness of what constitutes a responsible conversation and personal standards to adhere to throughout each conversation.

## The Way We Structure a Conversation Determines Its Success

Every conversation requires a structure. We need to know where
we are at every moment during the process of communicating.
Then we can stay on the path to our objective. The structure is

similar to a meeting agenda. Without an agenda, a meeting gets sidetracked by people with personal issues and concludes late, with participants frustrated and no goals reached.

The structure for every conversation includes four parts:

➤ Attention—the way I start a conversation to focus a listener's mind

➤ Benefits—the things I say that are important to the listener: pain or gain

➤ Resistance—the things the other person says that interrupt, disagree, or change the content

➤ Agreement—the question, statement, or action by the other person at the end of the conversation that tells me I have or have not achieved my objective

These four parts of the structure are divided into two sets of skills—speaking and listening. I know when I'm speaking (Attention, Benefits, Agreement). I know when I'm listening (Resistance).

Once we know these four structural parts and two skills, we can always locate ourselves in the conversation and be flexible by choosing the correct skill to use, moment by moment, depending on our objective and the responses of the other person.

## We Need to Relearn Two Essential Life Skills

| Skills |
|---|
| Responsible Listening |
| Responsible Speaking |

There are two sets of relearnable skills needed for conversations—responsible speaking and responsible listening. We are always either speaking or listening.

Unfortunately, only 5% of business people have ever taken a skill course in listening. Yet when asked to rate their effectiveness, most rate themselves at least 65% effective. Most of us think we are good listeners, yet 95% of us have no idea how to do it! In contrast, over 50% of business people have had some training in speaking—sales training, presentations, negotiations, or influencing skills. Unfortunately, most of these skills are taught with the idea of winning.

Although winning (achieving our objective) is important, what is essential in any responsible communication is to *establish trust* and *share information*. To achieve those two goals, we switch back and forth throughout the length of every conversation, between responsible listening and responsible speaking. Learning both may require a paradigm shift:

➤ The listening we do is actually the words we speak to prove to other people we understand what they are saying. Listening is not nodding or making eye contact. It's more complicated than that. It is saying, "I am not sure I understood what you said about ..."

➤ The speaking we do includes listening to be sure other people understand what we are saying. Speaking is not talking a lot, but also hearing people prove they understand us, at each point during the conversation.

When people know we understand them and we know they understand us, trust builds and information is shared.

## Our Communication System Sets Us Free

Peter Senge states in *The Fifth Discipline* that "a leader needs a communication system, which is what makes visible our limiting structures."

The intention of this book is

➤ to make visible to readers their limiting structures when they communicate,

➤ to confront each reader with an awareness of how difficult it is to communicate, and

➤ to provide a methodology for communicating responsibly, at work and at home.

> **System**
> Coaching
> (Listening)
> (Speaking)
> Declaring

Communications would be easy if people always treated each other with respect and were interested in sharing information rationally. However communications are not easy when people get emotional, either with themselves or with us. David Goleman, in his book *Emotional Intelligence*, states that emotions "short circuit" our ability to access rational information. Misunderstanding emotions puts relationships and information at risk.

In risky conversations, we need a system for understanding emotions. Then we need specialized types of listening and speaking if we are going to be 100% responsible for the quality of our conversations. Specialized speaking includes coaching people who are upset with themselves or others. It also includes declarative speaking, which is necessary when we are upset because people attack our characters or motivations. Knowing how to switch from one to the other at an appropriate time requires use of a system of communications.

The next chapter introduces and discusses the first of the four S's: Strategies—what we need to know before we start to speak or listen.

# CHAPTER 2

# Personal Strategies Keep Our Careers on a Fast Track

**W**ill Rogers once said, "The problem with people is not what they know. It's what they know that ain't so!"

**Strategies**

Awareness

What is "so" is that most of us have communication strategies that we use without knowing the effect they have on others. For example, many people have a strategy called "I always tell the truth." Sounds great! After all, either our parents or our church pastor taught us that. The problem is what our interpretation of the "truth" is. Telling someone the "truth" like "That is a dumb idea" or "Let me tell you how you should do that" is not the truth. It happens to be our *opinion*, an opinion the other person will have a difficult time accepting as the *truth*. The truth is facts that both people in a discussion can mutually understand.

Determining our strategies for conducting conversations responsibly requires two factors—awareness and standards. *Awareness* of the vital aspects of conversations helps us determine the quality of the conversations we choose to take part in. *Standards* allow us to stay in a conversation, whether comfortable or not, over a period of time needed to build trust and share information. In this chapter we'll focus on awareness, then move on to standards in Chapter 3.

## Awareness of Each Conversation

Five aspects of awareness require that we:

> **Awareness**
> 1. Strengths
> 2. Experiences
> 3. Beliefs
> 4. Quality of a Conversation
> 5. Roadblocks

➤ Confirm our personal communication strengths
➤ Clarify our personal life experiences
➤ Modify our personal communication beliefs
➤ Identify the quality of each conversation
➤ Eliminate major roadblocks to communication

If we choose to be most effective in one-on-one conversations, participating in or managing teams, making presentations, or selling products or ideas, then we must start with knowing ourselves. Our careers depend on it. We must confirm or acquire new self-knowledge, the knowledge necessary to play our strengths and minimize our vulnerabilities.

### We Start by Confirming Personal Strengths

We all know the adage, "Our greatest strength is our greatest weakness." For example, when asked the question, "What are your strengths when communi-

> **Awareness**
> 1. Strengths

cating?" people often say, "I'm direct, I get to the point, I'm passionate about what I say." Their response to the next question, "What communication habits have other people suggested that you change?", often is "I'm too blunt, too emotional." What a contrast! The person who is communicating directly is mentally saying, "Being direct and passionate is a good thing, it's a strength." The person who is listening is thinking, "This person is blunt, arrogant, his emotions are too strong." No wonder communication is not easy. We are so different!

Because we are so different, we need to use and respect our strengths. In most cases, our strengths are what has helped us be successful. However, we also need to recognize that 50% of the people we talk to may not appreciate our strengths—because their strengths are different.

For us to accept 100% responsibility for our communications, we need to confirm our strengths—and respect the strengths of others.

The beginning of being responsible is to complete a management motivational inventory. There are many validated, reliable motivational inventories on the market. If we have taken one, it maybe it's time to revisit it. If we have never taken one, it's essential to do so. Their results allow us to build new strategies for communicating effectively when we understand clearly, logically, and practically:

➤ How we communicate with others when we are doing what we like to do, free of constraints
➤ How we expect other people to communicate with us based on our learned behaviors
➤ What communication habits we may revert to when under emotional stress

The coaching story that follows indicates how an awareness of our strengths—and the strengths of others—may overcome the gap we can have in the way we communicate.

---

### What Does Diversity Mean to You?

His body and tone of voice gave off emotional reactions of anger and frustration. "As the human resource executive, I'm responsible for diversity and she has a whole department of women. No matter how much I talk to her, the next person she recruits ends up being the same!"

My response shocked him. "You really do not want diversity!"

His face got red and he defended by saying, "I do so! I'm committed to diversity."

"No, you are not," I replied. "You don't want any female managers who recruit other females."

The anger disappeared and was replaced by a sudden, thoughtful awareness.

"I get it now, about diversity, respecting diversity of people."

Part of a team-building effort we were conducting had included team members sharing the results of a motivational survey. Two of them seemed to be at extremes.

She was a person (not white, not female, just a human) who innately, genetically measured herself in terms of achieving short-term results, based on her practical, historical experiences. She was a financial officer who wanted immediate results: hire the first and best candidate who shows up.

He was a human resource executive motivated by gaining consensus and applying creative solutions to human problems. He wanted flexibility and time to look at a variety of candidates.

He and she had directly opposite motivations, totally opposite strengths. When they appreciated and understood each other's differences, communication improved and they could build trust and share information and hire a diverse workforce.

## What Are Our Strengths and Vulnerabilities?

Figure 2-1 shows a generalized summary of management style inventories that is useful in a simplistic way for indicating the variances among people and the importance of recognizing our styles. Thinking about the variances will help us begin to respect and communicate our differences.

Behaviors are divided into four categories—Action, People, Ideas, and Structure. The overriding differences among all four are how we process information and time. The two categories of Action and People require limited information and a short time frame. The two categories of Ideas and Structure require extensive information and a longer time frame. How we process time and information alone causes communications to be misinterpreted.

Read the four categories and select the two that most closely describe your motivations. This is a simplistic exercise, because

| Action | People |
|--------|--------|
| Direct | Diplomatic |
| Goal-Oriented | Responsive |
| Focused | Participatory |
| Energetic | Optimistic |
| Dependent | Adaptive |
| Authoritative | Consensual |
| Urgent | Inclusive |
| | Expansive |
| **Structure** | **Ideas** |
| Analytical | Information |
| Controlled | Probing |
| Autonomous | Supportive |
| Predictable | Conceptual |
| Orderly | Understanding |
| Consistent | Creative |
| Historical | Innovative |
| Organized | Continuous |

**Figure 2-1. A generalized summary of management behaviors**

we can access all four with different intensities, in different situations. But it will be useful to complete the exercises that follow.

Which two categories most sound like you?

_____Action _____People _____Structure _____Ideas

Which two categories describe someone who irritates you at work or at home?

_____Action _____People _____Structure _____Ideas

Usually the people who irritate us have different communication strengths. Usually the people we marry or live with have opposite strengths. We recognize the need for differences. We need the differences, particularly at work.

Our sales people who get paid by commission better be action-oriented, needing limited information or time. Our research people creating new products better be interested in new ideas, which require time and information to develop. We certainly want our accountants to be interested in structure, history, and numbers, which require time and information. Our human resource managers better be interested in people and building consensus.

## Personal Life Experiences Impact on Our Communications

Most of our communications are influenced by personal life experiences and particularly our responses when emotional and under stress. Since all communications are learned experiences, many of our responses are communications we learned at home responding to a parent or in school responding to teachers and coaches. When we become aware of how they influence our communications, we then can develop new strategies.

> **Awareness**
> 2. Experiences

One of the questions we need to answer is "What experiences do we think of when confronted with 'authority'?" As the following coaching story indicates, an individual at age 37 may still be operating out of a strategy developed by age 18.

### Our Experiences of Authority Affect Our Careers

A 37-year-old high-potential executive was sent to senior management for coaching on his presentation skills. He produced results, except in presentations, when senior managers would ask him a question. His responses provided lots of information but rarely ever directly answered the questions.

I asked him to tell me about his experiences with authority and a sad smile spread across his face.

So I asked, "Why are you smiling?"

He told me about a number of continuing experiences with authority. He started with his early years in a Catholic school where, if he didn't answer a question correctly, he got hit with a ruler. He told me about being questioned by the high school principal for cheating on papers he wrote because she didn't think he was that smart. He also received little support from his family, who always felt that the teachers and the principal must be right and then would punish him when he got home.

I asked him, "Are you telling me that when a senior manager asks you a question in a meeting, you're afraid you'll get punished if you don't give the right answer?"

He sheepishly smiled and said he thought so.

His old strategy was "to avoid answering a question directly so as not to get punished." I suggested a new strategy, "to answer every question directly and briefly." Then we spent two hours drilling ways to answer questions directly and briefly.

Two weeks later he came to our next meeting laughing. He told me that he had just made a presentation to senior management. He said, "I cut down the amount of information I gave them, which forced them to ask me questions. What I discovered was that by answering all their questions, I accomplished two things. I provided all the information I wanted them to have—and I looked smart doing it."

He learned a fundamental truth about communications. Communicating is giving people the information they want when they ask for it.

Besides authority, we have areas in our life and habits that are developed by our experiences growing up. A few include conflict, silence, and praise. When coaching, I ask people to complete the self-coaching questionnaire that follows. You may choose to do so as well. It can make you more aware of "things we know that just ain't so."

Each question is followed by examples of the responses two executives have given us. "A" was a senior financial officer; "B" was a research director. As you read each question, notice how different the responses are. Then there is a space for you to put your own response. When you finish the questionnaire, there will be some generalizations that will help you clarify your own experiences.

## Self-Coaching Questionnaire

1. What are your strengths when communicating?
   A. Passionate, direct, to the point.
   B. Good listener, insightful.
   Me:

2. What communication behaviors have others indicated you may wish to change?
   A. Too loud, interrupt people, opinionated.
   B. Aloof, snobbish, analyzes everything.
   Me:

3. Which communication behaviors used by three people important to your career (superior, peer, subordinate) irritate you the most?
   A. People who provide too much information, not specific.
   B. Angry, doesn't listen, babbles.
   Me:

4. What experience do you think of when you hear the word "authority"?
   A. People in command, fact of life, satisfy their agenda.
   B. Negative, teachers were insulting, anti-war protestor.
   Me:

5. How do you feel about conflict? Why?
   A. Necessary part of creative process, can be constructive: Taught conflict is useful.
   B. Doesn't like it, doesn't solve anything, no one yelled at home. Poor communications.
   Me:

6. What is your reaction, verbally and non-verbally, when confronted with silence (no feedback)?
   A. Maybe they don't understand; I didn't explain; I fill it with information.
   B. Make the other person comfortable, so I fill it.
   Me:

7. Are you comfortable giving/receiving praise? Why?
   A. Giving it, yes, receiving if it's specific. But don't need it.
   B. Giving it, OK, receiving it never—"Self-praise stinks."—Don't talk about self.

   Me:

Here are some ways to reflect on your responses to the self-coaching questionnaire:

➤ Usually what we perceive to be our strengths are what some people suggest that we change. Why? Different motivations.

➤ The people whose communication habits irritate us are people with opposite motivations. If we are direct and blunt, people who like to build consensus or provide voluminous information will irritate us.

➤ Our concept of authority may have a major impact on our communications. If we believe in authority and deem it necessary for getting things done, some people whom we manage will perceive us as "demanding," and even "demeaning," and "dictatorial." From this, they may learn that authority means not being very respectful of individuals.

➤ Most people handle conflict from two extremes—it's a fact of life, necessary for results, or it's destructive and irrational, to be avoided at all costs. If conflict is natural for us, people may perceive us as aggressive, provoking. If we avoid conflict, people may see us as passive, lacking confidence.

➤ Some people talk continually to fill silence. They believe that, if they provide us with sufficient information, we will hear something that will satisfy us. Other people are silent because they are methodically thinking about what we said and need time to evaluate it. Silence doesn't mean anything. People just handle it differently.

➤ Giving and receiving praise is a strong indication of self-worth. Those who can give praise may have grown up in an environment where people were acknowledged. Those who are uncomfortable receiving praise may have been taught "you can always do better," so nothing they do is good enough. It's important for managers to learn to give and receive praise.

The purpose of completing the questionnaire is to become more aware of many of our experiences that impact on our communications. Once we are aware of how we are all unique, we can be also more empathetic about people's differences. Chapters 4, 5, 6, 7, and 8 provide the communication skills necessary to maintain our strengths but communicate respectful of other people who have opposite strengths. When we become skilled communicators, we become like two-way radios on the same frequency: the words are clear. When we do not tune into another person's exact frequency, all we get is noise and static!

## Modifying Personal Beliefs Helps Eliminate Static

We all have religious, philosophical, moral, and ethical beliefs that we apply unconsciously to our communications with others. These beliefs we learned from parents, coaches, grandparents, friends, and

> **Awareness**
> 3. Beliefs

teachers. These beliefs that we carry within us describe how we "ought to" communicate with people.

Here are examples cited by executives in coaching sessions:

➤ "I tell the truth (brutally if necessary)."
➤ "I want you to trust me, be approachable and reliable."
➤ "Stand up for what you believe in."
➤ "I treat people the way I would like to be treated."

The coaching story just below demonstrates we may need to modify existing beliefs.

---

### I Have the Right to Speak Up ... or Do I?

One executive ended up in coaching because her superior thought she was bordering on being insubordinate. I asked her what her mother and/or father had taught her about authority or speaking up.

Her response: they had told her that the only thing important was to be able to express her mind. It didn't make any difference to whom she was speaking. If she didn't express her thoughts, no one would know what she thought and no one would know who she was.

---

> We then had a short discussion about making some distinctions about authority. I told her that I thought there were some people who had titles that were so important that they deserved respect in communications, no matter what, such as the President of the United States.
>
> I asked her what she thought about that.
>
> "That's something I hadn't considered," she replied.
>
> Her old strategy was "I have the right to speak up to anyone." We developed a new strategy: "I have the right to speak up to anyone, but should be respectful of knowledge and earned responsibility."

Here's an opportunity to review your beliefs and possibly make modifications. Listed below are examples of three executives' beliefs and the modifications they made. We attempted to keep their beliefs—but modify them to include respecting other people.

A. Old: I become passionate and intense to get results.
   New: I get results only when people understand what I say.

B. Old: I force people to take risks.
   New: People take risks when they trust me.

C. Old: Avoid being controlled by anyone.
   New: I keep control by communicating responsibly.

Why not list below two (or more) beliefs that you have that may not always work. How might you modify them now that you know how people might react? Changing the belief will help you change a communication behavior that may be a strength but an irritation to others.

1. Old:
   New:

2. Old:
   New:

Now that we have identified our strengths and personal beliefs, we can move on to identify the quality of each conversation we choose to take part in.

When a yellow flag is thrown in a football game, it indicates a rule violation. Play is stopped and an appropriate penalty is assessed against the violator.

Yellow flags (verbal or non-verbal) are thrown throughout most conversations. But what's interesting is that play continues and no penalties are assessed. Why? Because there are no agreed-upon rules for stopping the communication and assessing a penalty. Without agreed-upon rules, the quality of conversations can deteriorate rapidly because:

➤ We resist changing behavior.
➤ We justify own behavior.
➤ We stop communicating.

These behaviors cause an unequal conversation.

## Equal and Unequal Conversations

People immediately understand the difference between an *equal* conversation and an *unequal* conversation. An equal conversation reflects the following qualities:

| **Awareness** |
| --- |
| 4. Quality of a Conversation |
| • Equal |
| • Unequal |

Respectful                    Congruent
Trusting                      Rational

An unequal conversation reflects the opposite qualities:

Disrespectful                 Incongruent
Distrusting                   Emotional

A clearer way to describe an unequal conversation is to indicate the words, tone of voice, and gestures that exhibit superiority or attempt to control. These unequal statements usually are misuses of:

➤ *Power* (I'm the boss)—"Do it because I said so."
➤ *Knowledge* (I'm smarter)—"I know more than you do."
➤ *Emotions* (I'm the parent)—(angry) "You aren't serious, are you?"
➤ *Gestures* (I'm in charge)—finger pointing, etc.

Think back on a typical work day or week. What percentage of our conversations do we recognize as equal versus unequal? 25%-75%? 50%-50%? 75%-25%?

How an individual answers that question varies with the culture of his or her organization. Most people respond protectively at first and say, "75% equal, 25% unequal." I then ask them to include the conversations going on in their heads while they are judging what other people say—non-verbal conversations like "Who does he think he is, talking to me like that?" or "I wish she'd stop talking so much and let me speak." The percentages then quickly change to 50%-50% or even 25% equal, 75% unequal.

Any conversation, whether verbal or non-verbal, can become an unequal conversation, because an unequal conversation is one in which information and relationships are being strained. It's hard to share information when the other person is giving off signs of impatience, interrupting us, or saying, "I'm the boss" or "I know more than you do!" or "You aren't serious, are you?"

When I enter into a conversation, I'm first listening for the quality of the conversation. Is it equal or unequal? If it's unequal, I prepare for a longer, more difficult conversation, one in which information and relationship may be at risk, one in which I need to accept 100% responsibility to skillfully help the conversation become equal.

Now that you know what makes a conversation unequal, think back on one you were in recently. What did you or the other person say or think that made it unequal? What did either of you say or think to make it equal? List below what you remember.

## Unequal Conversation

(Statements, gestures, tone of voice, thoughts)

1.

2.

3.

4.

## Equal Conversation

(Statements, gestures, tone of voice, thoughts)

1.

2.

3.

4.

Now that you can recognize the differences between equal and unequal conversations, let's get specific. What is in the content of the unequal conversation that blocks our willingness to communicate? There are the three major roadblocks to communications.

# We Have to Recognize Major Roadblocks to Communications

Most of us do not realize that many of our statements, questions, and actions communicate lack of acceptance of the other person and make him or her less willing to allow the conversation to move forward. Most of these unaccepting communications block communications because they are double messages: they say one thing and imply another. The implied message usually:

> **Awareness**
> 5. Roadblocks
>    • Judgments
>    • Solutions
>    • Justifications

➤ Makes an evaluation or judgment of the other person's character or motives.
➤ Gives our solution to the other person's problem.
➤ Justifies our behaviors.

We need to be able to identify these roadblocks—when we create them or when other people create them.

### We Are Judgment Machines

Our learned habits are to judge other people's characters and motives. What we do is force people to defend their actions rather than consider alternate solutions. We make these judgments, verbally and

> **Roadblock 1**
> Judgments

nonverbally, in ways similar to the following:

"You were discourteous in our staff meeting."
"You act like a know-it-all."
"You used our meeting to show off how smart you are."

Are you willing to try a Herculean feat that will result in new freedom?

Keep a list of judgments you hear in the next few conversations. Mentally jot down judgment words that you hear other people or that you use. "She is shy" … "He lacks initiative" ... "You're the problem" … "You're pretty" … "Why do you act so negatively?"… "You're not listening." ... "You are doing it wrong again."

After listening to the conversations, go into your office, close the door, and review the list. None of these judgments are true. They are only someone's opinion!

So here's where the newfound freedom comes in! Judgments are *generalizations*, not *specifics*. They are *opinions*, not *truths*. As one executive I was coaching said, "You mean I no longer have to justify my actions?" Bingo! Now we can focus on moving from judgments to gathering information we need. Sample ways to do that might be:

➤ "I didn't realize I sounded stupid. It would be helpful if you could provide specifics so I can understand why you are calling me stupid."

➤ "I didn't know you felt I was stupid. Thanks for telling me. Now could we move ahead to the problem at hand?"

When we hear other people's judgments as their opinions, we are free to prove that we heard them and not attack, justify, or defend; we can then move on to explore the facts. Not being a "judgment machine" saves enormous time and energy!

Here's a story to drive home the point.

---

### "She's Shy." "No, She's Aggressive."— How Do We Know the Difference?

One day I was holding my 18-month-old granddaughter.
My son said to me, "She's shy."

My response was "I think she's aggressive." A shocked look appeared on his face.

I asked him, "What do you mean by 'shy'?"

His response was "She doesn't talk very much."

I said, "You're right, she doesn't talk very much."

He smiled, then asked, "What do you mean by 'aggressive'?"

My response: "Whenever people talk to her, she looks them right in the eyes."

We started with different labels to describe the same child. We ended up with behavior descriptions we both understood and could agree to.

Often in workshops I will ask, "How many people in this room have grown up with a label given to them as a child?" Many people put up their hands. Then I ask them, "How many of you asked what people meant by it?" Very few respond.

Most children go through life living out a label. The skill for avoiding labels is to describe the label in terms of behavior. If my son said to his daughter, "You don't talk a lot," they could have a conversation about how much, why, and what to do.

There's not very much she could do about being shy.

We need to be 100% responsible to stop judging other people in our conversations, verbally and mentally. There is no truer statement than "Judge not lest you be judged." The moment we judge someone's character, the conversation becomes unequal and that person stops listening. We force him or her to be defensive or to attack.

Here's an opportunity to practice eliminating judgments. I've given an example of a judgment statement used in performance reviews, followed by an example of how it might be made specific:

**Statement:** Pete, you need to show more initiative.

**Specific:** Pete, you need to show more initiative. By initiative, I mean you need to ask relevant questions in each meeting.

List below at least two judgment words you may be using with a specific subordinate or two judgment words you have heard senior management use with you or others. Then define them in terms of specific behaviors that anyone listening would understand.

| Judgment Word | Specific Description |
|---|---|
| 1. | |
| 2. | |

Eliminating our use of judgment words and not defending against them when people label us will be a lifetime task. From now on, you will be shockingly aware of how much judgment goes on in conversations. We may not be able to control others, but we can be responsible for our own side of the conversation.

## Praise—Roadblock or Motivator

An important management skill is an ability to praise subordinates. Most executives have read books suggesting that praise is an important empowerment tool, but many are uncomfortable doing it. If we are uncomfortable giving or receiving praise, these coaching stories may help.

---

### Learning to Give Praise Is Essential, But Not Easy!

I had an executive referred to me because she was "tough" on her subordinates and had excessive turnover in her department. According to her manager, "She never praises anyone. All she does is criticize."

In my first session with her, I asked, "How are you in terms of giving and receiving praise?"

She responded, "I never give praise. People can always do better than they've done."

I asked her where she got that particular philosophy.

Her response: "No matter what grade I got in school, my parents always said I could do better."

"So you never received any praise at home? Is that what you're telling me?"

"Yes."

"OK," I said, "we're going to try an experiment here. I'm going to praise you, and I'd like you to at least say, 'Thank you.'"

She looked at me with a strange, almost angry stare. Then I made a true statement to her.

---

I said, "I want you to know that in the short time we've been together you've learned this material presented faster than most of the people I've worked with."

"Well," she responded, "I don't think that's true."

"Stop! I've asked you just to acknowledge and accept the praise. All you have to do is say, "Thank you.' Now, we are going to do the drill again." I repeated the statement.

"Thank you," she replied—and her face turned deep red. It was the first time that she could remember ever allowing a compliment to sink in.

Another praise story involved the chairman of a major consulting company.

## A New Definition for a Type A Personality— "I Can Always Do Better."

Early in our coaching meeting, I asked him, "What is the one communication problem or opportunity you'd like to handle in this half-day session?"

He said, "I can't stand it when our new MBAs try to impress me with how smart they are. They read one article and then try to impress me with their knowledge. I beat them up. I'd like to know how to stop doing that. "

"That's easy," I said. "Can I assume you came from a family where praise was not given?"

"Yes, I was always expected to do better. I never received any compliments."

"OK," I said. "I'm going to send you two messages of praise. I want you to hold your responses until I send you both. Then I'll ask you which one was more acceptable to you.

"OK!"

"Praise #1: You've done a great job as chairman of this company."

"Praise #2: You've done a great job as chairman of this company. In the five years of existence, you've taken the company from nothing to fifteen million a year. You now help feed the families of over 150 people, and this year you were written up in major publications as the consulting company that attracts the most MBAs to compete for limited openings."

> "Which praise could you accept?"
> "The second!"
> "Why?"
> "Because it was specific. I could decide for myself whether I believed you or not."

Because giving and receiving praise is an important motivational tool—when not judgmental—I ask workshop participants to practice giving praise. Below are the phrases I ask them to complete with their partner. You might want to try them with a family member, a subordinate, or even your manager. When delivered with specifics, we all may accept praise—gratefully!

I want to thank you for_____(Be specific!)_____.
I appreciate you for_____(Be specific!)_____.
I value what you did because _____(Be specific!)_____.
I respect that you _____(Be specific!)_____.

Now that you may be able to give praise without making it a judgment, how are you when receiving or giving a gift? Have you ever given a gift to someone and had him or her say, "I don't want it" or "You don't have to do that"?

It's not an unusual reaction. For many people, accepting a gift is an uncomfortable experience. It's like accepting what they believe is unwarranted praise. It's uncomfortable for some people who have very high expectations for their standards of performance. Other people are uncomfortable with gifts because they have low self-esteem. As children they may have repeatedly been told, "You don't deserve good grades. Your work isn't good enough."

## "I Don't Want Your Gift."

Giving and receiving gifts has become an affectionate game between my daughter-in-law and me. Early in our relationship, when we gave her a gift she'd respond, "You don't have to do that" or "We really don't need it; it's not necessary."

One day we had the following conversation after she had attempted to decline a gift.

> "I want to ask you a question," I said. "If a friend of yours came to your house one night and gave you an unexpected gift, how would you feel?"
>
> "Uncomfortable."
>
> "Would you say to her, 'I don't want it, take it back'?"
>
> "Of course not," she responded.
>
> "OK," I said. "When we send you a gift and you tell us you don't need it or it's not necessary, I feel like you're giving me the gift back."
>
> Since that conversation, I have become aware of how often I do the same thing. She playfully reminds me, when I resist a gift she sends, "I feel like you're giving the gift back."
>
> Next time someone praises you, consider it a gift. Will you tell them you don't want it? Or will you accept it in the spirit it was given?

## We Love to Give Solutions—and People Resist Them

Next to judging someone's character or motivations, giving unrequested solutions to other people's problems is a major roadblock to equal conversations.

**Roadblock 2**
Solutions

Can you recall a recent conversation in which someone at work or at home told you what to do?

"That won't work. Let me tell you how to do it."
"I wouldn't let a subordinate get away with that. If I were you, I'd ..."
"Your job is to listen, not participate."

Solution messages that people deliver to us, particularly in an unequal way and when we haven't asked for help, shift our energy from solving our own problems to considering other solutions—and they stir up our emotions. The underlying message is that the other person is smarter than we are. In most cases, we've already considered their solution and discarded it or they provide us with information we already know, which is an insult to our intelligence.

Jot down in the space below two solutions recently given to you. How did the person give them? Had you already considered the solution? What conversation did you have in your head?

1. Statement made to you:
   Solution:
   Your feelings/thoughts:

2. Statement made to you:
   Solution:
   Your feelings/thoughts:

---

### When We Give "Solutions," People Don't Listen

I received a solution message in a recent coaching session with a plant manager in a Spanish speaking country. I asked the plant manager, "What comments have other people made to you about your communications?"

"My wife says I 'give speeches,'" he answered. Although he disagreed with her, he had moments before demonstrated his speech giving in his conversation with me. He had given me a lecture on why there were misconceptions about him because of a misunderstanding by people in his plant of his use of a personal pronoun in Spanish. For my education he comprehensively detailed the difference.

When he finished, I said to him, "Your wife is right. You do give speeches."

"What do you mean?" he asked.

I said, "You gave me an extended lecture on the use of a personal pronoun in Spanish."

"Yes," he said. "I wanted to help you to understand."

"I stopped listening after your first sentence."

"Why?"

"Because I took four years of Spanish in high school," I answered. "I knew exactly what you were talking about and you were wasting my time and insulting my intelligence. You were giving me a solution for something I knew."

He sat quietly.

I said to him, "Thanks for teaching me a new definition for the word 'speech.' A speech is when you give someone a solution for something they already know."

> "How can I avoid doing that?"
>
> "Ask a question before you launch into a lecture. What question could you have asked?"
>
> "Peter, do you speak any Spanish?"

One way to avoid being perceived as harsh or bullying (the reasons the plant manager was referred for coaching) is to never give information until you discover how much the person or group knows about the subject.

What is also important to know about people who give us solutions is that they do it because:

➤ They desire to help us.

➤ They are self-critical and are attempting to ensure the effectiveness of their own performance.

We can afford to be patient with people who are punishing themselves.

## We Are Justification Addicts!

Justifying our behavior is the third major roadblock to communications. We have spent a lifetime addicted to justifying our behavior to others, to prove we are right and they are wrong. (It was one way to maintain our self-esteem when under attack by parents, teachers, and coaches.)

> **Roadblock 3**
> Justifications

Do any of the following justifications sound like things that you have said or that others have said to you?

"I did it because you made me do it."

"After twenty years of experience, I ought to know what I'm doing."

"I just did what everyone else was doing."

When was the last time, at work or at home, you justified an action of yours? Here is an exercise to experience communicating, not justifying. Jot down below two recent conversations in

## We Never Need to Justify Our Behavior

I had a great opportunity to justify my behavior one day in a conversation with my wife.

She started by saying, "You don't respect our garbage men!"

What an insult! I'm an early riser and at least three days a week I have coffee with them, since we all go to the only delicatessen in town that opens at 6:00 a.m. I know most of them by name. Often I'll pick one up who is walking to the delicatessen. But I had a choice to make: justify or communicate.

I said, "Tell me why you think that."

"You put our bottles and cans in plastic bags and then they have to empty them. Then they put the bags back in our driveway. It's an extra process for them and our driveway is a mess!"

"Would you like to know why I do that?" I asked her quietly.

"No," she answered me.

"OK," I said. "Thanks for telling me that."

The conversation ended amicably. She had expressed her opinion. I had listened to it. My choice was to justify or to do something with the information.

I was tempted to justify and say, "What gives you the right to tell me I don't respect the garbage men? I have coffee with them every day, I know their names, etc, etc, etc."

But by listening to her, I was free to make a choice. By listening, I can change my behavior because I choose to—not because I am forced to—and I don't have to burn up energy justifying my behavior.

which you justified your position. Then list the response you made in each situation. What other choices could you have made?

| Situation | Choices |
|---|---|
| 1. | 1. |
| 2. | 2. |

When we realize we always have choices of ways to respond, we can reduce or eliminate our justifications. With choices, we can lick our addiction to justifications.

## Summary of Awareness

"The problem with people is not what they know. It's what they know that ain't so." What we now know is we need strategies that allow us to be aware of what will happen in any conversation. Awareness includes:

| Awareness |
|---|
| 1. Strengths |
| 2. Experiences |
| 3. Beliefs |
| 4. Quality of a Conversation |
| 5. Roadblocks |

➤ Knowing our personal communication strengths and respecting those of others

➤ Recognizing how our personal experiences (authority, conflict, silence) affect our communications

➤ Changing some of our beliefs ("I tell the truth") to respect others ("The truth is what other people understand I mean")

➤ Identifying whether I'm in an unequal conversation ("I'm the boss," "I'm smarter") or not

➤ Eliminating major roadblocks (judgments, solutions, justifications)

### Next Step

Now that we know what to be aware of, we need to develop our own standards of communication behaviors.

# CHAPTER 3

# Personal Strategies Provide Standards to Control Each Conversation

*O*nce we determine the quality of each conversation we are in, we need personal standards to control the quality.

I start a workshop by walking over to a participant and saying, "I'd like to have a brief conversation with you from which you will benefit, as well the rest of the participants. Are you willing?"

With his agreement, I ask him, "If we're going to have a conversation, I'd like to know before we start what rules or standards you will use throughout."

Sometimes he'll hesitate, surprised by the question. Sometimes he may respond, "I'll treat you professionally."

My response is a question: "What do you mean by *professionally*?"

At that point I thank him and turn to the audience and say, "If I want to be responsible for the quality of my conversations, I need to decide *before* I *start* each conversation what personal standards I will use throughout the conversation."

> **Standards**
> • Objective
> • Time
> • Exits
> • Skills

There are four general standards that we might consider when determining our personal set of standards:

➤ Decide on a specific *objective* for each conversation
➤ Determine the expected *time length* for each conversation
➤ Choose options to be used to *exit* or terminate the conversation
➤ Commit to using *responsible skills* throughout

## A Specific Objective for Each Conversation Aims at Our Goal

Any well-run meeting has an agenda that's distributed in advance so people know what to expect and can plan their participation. Even with it, a skilled meeting manager has to remind people to stay on the agenda if they are to achieve the goals of the meeting.

> **Standards**
> • Agenda
> • Question
> • Statement

*A conversation is a meeting between two people*. At the start of a conversation, I immediately state my objective and ask for agreement: "Charlie, thank you for meeting with me today. At the end of this meeting, I'd like to have us agree to a scheduled date for a team-building workshop next month for you and your staff."

People respond differently when they hear that approach— "too direct," "almost rude," "selfish," "great, I like it," and "clear and direct."

Responsible communications is not about being liked. It's about making decisions, selling ideas and concepts, building relationships, managing people, and contributing our personal ability and knowledge. Without clear, specific objectives for a conversation, personal agendas can sidetrack the conversation so that both people end the conversation unsatisfied.

*What is an objective for a conversation?* An objective is what the *other person will do* at the end of the conversation; it is what you want him or her to commit to doing. It is when the other person:

➤ Makes a statement—"Let's schedule the team-building session for the first Tuesday next month."

➤ Asks a question—"If we schedule it for next month, what preliminary arrangements do we have to make?"

➤ Takes an action—"I'll have my assistant send out the announcement tomorrow."

An objective is specific, numerical, and ambitious: "Charlie, at the end of this meeting, let's agree to a scheduled date next month for a team-building session."

An objective is not what we will do. It is defined in terms of what the *other person will do*. An objective would not be "Charlie, I'd like to make a presentation to you about the value of doing a team-building workshop." Anybody can make a presentation! An objective is not a presentation. An objective is achieved when the other person agrees or disagrees *to do what we request*.

---

## Have You Had to Change Objectives in the Middle of a Conversation?

One night I walked into the kitchen, upset with something my wife had done. She was standing at the sink with her back to me. I started the conversation this way:

"You know that last discussion we had. I didn't like the way you talked to me in that conversation."

The response I got was disagreement. I realized in the middle of her defense that the way I had started the conversation certainly indicated the wrong objective. If my objective in the conversation was to tell her how dumb she was, then I got the exact results I could expect—defensiveness and an attack on me.

So I interrupted her and I said, "Let me start over again. I think this conversation will take five minutes. At the end of this conversation, I would like to be able to know exactly what I said that bothered you; I'd like to be able to tell you why I said what I said. At the end of the conversation, let's see if we can come to some agreement so we'll both treat each other with respect in future conversations."

The lesson I keep forgetting in conversations, particularly personal and/or emotional conversations, is to *start with the factual end result and state that up front.* That way we both can come to an agreement at the start on what the end result will be.

To confirm your understanding of what an objective is, consider a recent conversation you had, particularly one that may not have worked out the way you wanted. If you could do the conversation over again, what would your objectives be? Use the format that follows.

**Original Objective**                                   **New Objective**
*(What I would do)*                                      *(What statement,*
                                                         *action, or question*
                                                         *he or she would*
                                                         *make, take, or ask)*

1.

2.

Setting an objective doesn't take long. We can do it walking down the hall to someone's office or in a moment before we pick up the telephone to make a call.

## Different People Set Different Time Limits for Each Conversation

Once we know our objective for a conversation, we need to determine a specific length of time for the conversation. Different people are willing to commit different amounts of time to any given conversation. When a conversation starts, an action-oriented person wants the conversation to be *brief, to the point, and over quickly*—so he or she can get a result. A thoughtful, idea-oriented person expects the conversation to be as *long as necessary* to exchange sufficient information to get a creative substantive result. Unless the two people mutually agree and commit to a time span *at the beginning of the conversation*, both people

**Standards**
Time Limit
• Start
• Change
• Shorten

listen and speak on their own wavelengths. If no commitment is made, static then prevails: information is inaccurate and relationships get strained.

Here's how an *ineffective* conversation might start between two people who process time and information differently:

**Action-oriented person:** "Give me no more than two points—so we can decide now."

**Idea-oriented person:** "It's not that simple. I've read two studies on this matter, and we need to discuss their findings in depth so we can make the right decision!"

Here's how an *effective* conversation might start between an action person and an idea person.

**Action-oriented person:** "I've got five minutes to spend before we make a decision."

**Idea-oriented person:** "I'd like ten minutes to make sure essential information is shared."

**Action-oriented person:** "Split the difference. Seven and a half."

**Idea-oriented person:** "OK, but at seven and a half we may need to agree to extend the meeting or schedule additional time later."

If we expect people to stay in a communication with us to the end, we need to initially agree to a time frame. Without agreement, the quality of the information exchanged may be poor and the strain on the relationship will increase.

*But what do we do when other people initiate the conversation and no time frame is set?* I listen intently for a brief period of time, then make a verbal or non-verbal decision about how long I expect to be in the conversation. I do this so I will not be guilty of what most of us think we can do—doing two things at one time.

---

### People Can Think About Only One Thing at a Time

James Stewart taught that principle in the movie *Carbine Williams*. As part of a punishment when in prison for "moonshining," he was put in the hole, a cramped position where a man could not lie down or stand up. The pain is so great that most people are severely damaged by the time they come out. Not Stewart—he stretched and walked out!

How did he do that? He said the pain was great at first. Then he realized the mind can do only one thing at a time. So he spent his time mentally creating the first automatic rifle rather than focusing on the pain.

Sometimes listening to people who talk too long, ramble, and get off the agenda is as painful as being put in the hole. But if we determine a specific time we think the conversation will take, we can stay focused so we can be 100% responsible for the results of the conversation.

## Changing the Time Limit of a Conversation, Moment by Moment

During a conversation I may change my commitment to how long I'll stay focused. At the beginning of the conversation, I may have committed to 15 minutes. As the conversation progresses, I may decide:

**Standards**
Time Limits
• Change

➤ Information and/or relationship do not require as much time
➤ Information and/or relationship require longer time

At the time I make that decision, I verbally commit to a new time. Here are two examples:

"After discussing this for the past five minutes, I think I need to complete this shortly. Can we summarize or focus on the two essential points? If not, I need to reschedule so I can give you my full attention."

"After discussing this for the past five minutes, I think the information/problem will require more time to solve to our satisfaction. Do you have an additional twenty minutes? Or should we reschedule?"

Does that sound rude? Maybe. Or is it ruder to mentally decide that the conversation isn't worth it and to start reading papers on my desk or solving a different problem—while the person is still talking?

One way or the other, the conversation is over if we do not agree to change the time limit. It may end because one of us decides we've spent enough time. When that happens, the person will tune out, stop listening, and start doing something else. When the second person recognizes that the first has left the conversation, he or she may get upset, speak longer, and repeat what we already have discussed.

With no agreed time frame, effective conversations are difficult.

## We Have a Right to Exit Difficult Conversations

Even when we have set an objective and agreed to a time frame, we periodically need to extricate ourselves from difficult conversations, conversations during which the other person attacks us or talks to us in a way that seems unethical, treatment that we do not appreciate (severely unequal conversations).

> **Standards**
> Exits
> • Silence
> • Leave
> • Help

We need to be able to exit the conversation by *stopping* the other person, *leaving* the room, or *asking* for help.

The coaching story that follows requires no theoretical support. The actions described are obviously risky and courageous. But not to choose one is even riskier. If we fight back, others in the room watch the fight and forget the content. If the other person dominates us, insults us, others in the room question our strengths. If we become passive, people wonder about our self-confidence.

---

### How Would You Respond to Someone Who Says to You, "Shut Up and Listen!"?

Twice, on the same day, two executives, from two companies, from two states, asked me the same question: "How do you respond to someone in a meeting who says to you, 'Shut up and listen!'?"

There is no easy answer, especially when that person in one case is the president of the company and in the other case is a peer in a cross-functional meeting, a peer with whom you compete for resources and decisions.

When someone attacks us in an unequal conversation, we need to know we do have a choice. We can attack, defend, or communicate. The best communication might be to exit the conversation.

I asked the executive whose peer had told him to "shut up and listen" how he had responded.

He said, "I told him, 'No, you shut up and listen.'"

Then I asked, "At that point, did the meeting move forward or were the rest of the participants watching the fight, picking sides?"

He answered with a question: "What are you supposed to do when someone attacks you?"

My answer: "Make a choice from exit strategies."

When we are under personal attack, a strong silent response is a possibility. Get up quietly and leave the meeting. Say nothing. No one has a right to attack our self-esteem publicly.

Another executive with whom I had discussed the same issue did exactly that. He got up and left the room.

I asked him, "What was the reaction from the others?"

"No one ever said a word," he said, "in the meeting or afterwards. It was like it never happened—and the individual never yelled again."

Another silent response would be to do just what was asked. Be silent. Shut up and listen. Look at the executive in a focused, confident way and say nothing to him again—for the rest of the meeting. Respond to no further statements or discussions throughout the meeting, even if asked, but be intently interested. Silence may be the most powerful tool we have. People often get very uncomfortable—even feeling guilty—when we do exactly as they ask! If someone asked why you were not taking part, the answer would be "I was told to shut up and listen."

A third possibility is to turn to the meeting manager and say, "I need your help. I'm not accustomed to being talked to like that. I'll find it difficult to remain here if I'm attacked again."

That story is dramatic and an extreme. But the principle is the same. We always have choices we can make that allow us to maintain our self-esteem—and not attack the other person in an unequal way.

However, the best way to not have to exit a conversation is to practice and master the skills of *responsible listening* and *responsible speaking*.

## I Am 100% Responsible to Listen and Speak

When I enter a conversation with another person, I accept 100% of the responsibility for the quality of the conversation.

| Standards |
|---|
| Responsible Skills |
| • Speaking |
| • Listening |

Why do I accept 100% responsibility when I know that "it takes two to tango"?

I take responsibility because I'm studying and developing communications strategies and skills so I know where I am in a conversation. Most people are unaware of their strategies and have never practiced skills, so they have no idea where they are in a conversation. Why would I want to share responsibility with an unskilled partner, to start a 50-50 venture?

For me to be responsible for the quality of a conversation, there are two fundamental skills required—speaking and listening. What never ceases to amaze me is the ability of people to immediately improve their skills of speaking and listening *just by committing to being 100% responsible* for using those skills in each conversation.

---

### What Will You Do Differently Next Time?

At the beginning of a coaching session or a workshop, I'll ask participants to do three things.

First, I ask them to focus on a recent conversation with an individual at work or at home that didn't go as well as they wished. (You might want to do that now.) What did they say? What did you say? What didn't you like about the results?

Once people have in mind a recent conversation, I ask this question: "If you had been willing to be 100% responsible for understanding what the other person said, no matter how poorly he or she said it, how would you have listened differently?"

People have no problem identifying how they would have listened differently.

> ➤ "I would have asked more questions."
> ➤ "I would not have interrupted them as much."
> ➤ "I would give up all judgments I had about how dumb they were."

If you could replay your recent conversation that didn't go well, what would you do differently so you would be 100% responsible to understand what the other person said? How would you *listen differently*?

1.

2.

Next I ask the workshop participants this question: "If you had been willing to be 100% responsible that the person understood what you said, no matter how poorly he or she listened, how would you have *spoken differently*?"

Immediate responses include:

> ➤ "I would have given less information."
> ➤ "I would have asked if they understood me."
> ➤ "I would not have raised my voice when I got impatient."

How would you *speak differently* in that conversation if you had another chance to be 100% responsible that the person understood what you said?

1.

2.

## Summary of Standards

Tolstoy said, "Everyone thinks about changing humanity but no one thinks about changing himself." Developing our personal set of standards allows us to change our communications and—without trying—we will help the other person be more responsible for his or her side of the conversation.

I change my conversations, instituting standards that:

> ➤ Require each conversation to have an end objective—a statement, question, or action by the other person that lets me know I've reached my goal.
> ➤ Set a time limit, verbally or nonverbally, for the length of each

conversation, so I can stay focused on our interactions and not try to do two things at once.

➤ Plan exits from difficult conversations, so I protect my self-esteem and refrain from attacking, defending, or justifying.

➤ Accept 100% responsibility for listening to people so I understand them and for speaking to them so they will understand me.

# Strategies

### Rating of Ability to Identify the Quality of a Conversation and Apply Standards

For each fundamental listed below, plase an "X" at the point you rate your mastery of that fundamental (1 is lowest, 10 is highest.) Repeat this procedure periodically.

### Awareness of the Quality of Each Conversation

1. I am aware of my strengths (motivations)—action, people, idea, structure.  1 .......................................................... 10
2. I know how conflict affects communications.  1 .......................................................... 10
3. I know how authority affects communications.  1 .......................................................... 10
4. I know how I handle silence.  1 .......................................................... 10
5. I am aware of equal and unequal conversations.  1 .......................................................... 10
6. I have reduced my use of character judgments.  1 .......................................................... 10
7. I have reduced giving people solutions to their problems.  1 .......................................................... 10
8. I justify my behavior less.  1 .......................................................... 10

## Standards Applied to Each Conversation

1. I have a precise objective
   before I start a conversation.        1 ................................................ 10
2. I agree to a set time limit to
   each conversation.                    1 ................................................ 10
3. I know how to exit difficult
   conversations.                        1 ................................................ 10
4. I listen responsibly 100% of
   the time.                             1 ................................................ 10
5. I speak responsibly 100% of
   the time.                             1 ................................................ 10

# CHAPTER 4

# Every Conversation Needs a Flexible Structure

*T*here are four S's to Responsible Communications. *Strategies* we've just finished. *Structuring* a conversation is the second S in the communication process.

**600-Word Gap**

Why is structuring every conversation important? Because when I speak to another person, physically I can speak at a rate of only 150 to 250 words per minute. Someone listening to me can physically listen to 750 to 1000 words a minute. Obviously there is a time and information gap.

A *structured* conversation is used to bridge the 600-word gap between *reality and fantasy. Reality* is what I'm saying at a slow speed. *Fantasy* is what the listener hears and thinks about in the same period of time.

The coaching story that follows is indicative of what happens to our communications when we lack any predetermined structure.

---

### What Do You Think of When You Hear the Word *Volunteer*?

I demonstrate the gap between fantasy and reality, this 600-word gap, at the beginning of many workshops.

I start by asking for a volunteer: "I need a volunteer."

I do it with a slightly raised tone of voice, sounding authoritative, and I raise my right hand and point upward.

Silence! 99% of the time no one volunteers.

Then I ask, "What were the conversations going on in your heads when you heard the word *volunteer*?"

Laughter starts to ripple across the room with answers like:

"Not me, I volunteer Jim!" (pointing at another participant)

"You have to be crazy! In front of all these people?"

"I volunteered once in the army!"

"My mother didn't raise no fool!"

After gathering this information, I say, "The real question is not who will volunteer but who in this room can tell me what was my physical gesture and what was my tone of voice when I said, 'I need a volunteer'?"

(Silence!)

---

The reason most people miss the tone of voice and physical gesture is because their minds run faster than I can talk. It is into this 600-word gap that most people race when they hear a hot word such as "volunteer," "abortion," "Republican," etc. Their imaginations pull up old experiences and in the process they do not pay attention to the speaker's tone of voice or physical gestures.

What is more interesting is that extensive communication research indicates that words carry no more than 7% of our message. Tone of voice and particularly facial gestures are 75% of the message. Most of us miss 75% of the message because we don't have a structure that will limit our fantasies.

What helps us listen and speak reality is a structured conversation that has

➤ four parts
➤ two set of skills
➤ flexibility

The structured model that we are about to explore is a universally accepted one that marketing, sales, and advertising executives use daily.

## There Are Four Parts to Each Conversation

The structure of all responsible conversations includes four parts:

> | **Structure** |
> | Four Parts |
> | • Attention |
> | • Benefits |
> | • Resistance |
> | • Agreement |

➤ Attention—the way I start a conversation to focus a listener's mind
➤ Benefits—the things I say that are important to the listener: pain or gain
➤ Resistance—the things the other person says that interrupt, disagree, or change the content
➤ Agreement—the question, statement, and/or action the other person or I ask, make, or take that tells me I have achieved or not achieved the objective of the conversation

## We Need Two Sets of Special Communication Skills

All four of these parts are learnable communication skills. Three of them are used when I'm speaking (attention, benefits, agreement) and one is used when I'm listening (acknowledging and asking questions.)

> | **Structure** |
> | Two Skills |
> | • Responsible Speaking |
> | • Responsible Listening |

The two sets of skills look like this:

**Responsible Speaking** → Attention *Focus* → Benefits *Pain or Gain* → Agreement *Question Statement Action*

**Responsible Listening** → Acknowledge *Ask Questions Reduce Resistance*

Once we know how a conversation is structured, we need to be flexible in the way we use the structured parts.

## Staying Flexible Is the Name of the Game

In the figure at the right showing two models of a conversation, model 1 may look unstructured and even confusing. You read that a structured conversation had four parts—attention, benefits, resistance, and agreement. You may have thought the conversation logically starts at attention and finishes with agreement, as with model 2.

No. What is structured is that there are only four parts, which are taught in two skills (speaking and listening). The power to this structure is its flexibility. A structured conversation has to be flexible, because we have no idea how the other person will respond or when.

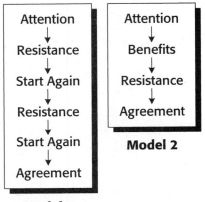

**Communication is a flexible process consisting of *Speaking + Listening***

Attention
↓
Resistance
↓
Start Again
↓
Resistance
↓
Start Again
↓
Agreement

**Model 1**

Attention
↓
Benefits
↓
Resistance
↓
Agreement

**Model 2**

Model 1 indicates that I start a conversation and get an immediate response from the other person—a question, a change of agenda, a request to have the conversation at another time (resistance). What model 1 indicates is a flexible use of the four parts, depending on the reactions of the other person.

The conversation that follows may solidify your understanding of a flexible but structured conversation.

---

### When We Sell an Idea, Give Them a Choice— The Long Version or the Short Version

A few years ago I called on a prospective client to discuss an executive development coaching process. He was 30 minutes late for our scheduled appointment. He apologized and commented on his busy schedule. I started the conversation this way:

*Attention*—"Bob, because you are busy,

*Benefit*—can I assume you'd like the short version rather than the long one?"

*Resistance*—(Said with appreciation, animation, and a sense of relief) "I'd love the short version!"

*Benefit*—"The short version is what you'll get.

*Agreement*—When will you send us the first candidate for coaching?"

*Resistance*—(He laughed.) "That's too short!"

*Attention*—"If that's too short, I'd like to ask you three questions.

*Benefits*—And if you answer them, we'll be gone in fifteen minutes."

*Resistance*—(With complete agreement) "What are the three questions?"

*Attention*—"Which competitors do you use?
            —What programs do you hire them to perform?
            —How much do they charge?"

*Resistance*—(With a soft smile) "I'll answer the first two, not the third."

*Attention*—"Great, if you'll answer those two questions, I'll tell you how different we are.

*Benefit*—We'll be gone in fifteen minutes."

The rest of the conversation consisted of brief exchanges of information and we left with him agreeing to try us. From my viewpoint, it was a very *structured, flexible* conversation. I always knew which skill I was using in response to his reactions. I used this flexible approach with him because he was a senior vice president and had some gray hair, a sense of humor, and self-confidence. I was willing to ask for agreement ("When will you send us the first candidate for coaching?") *without* giving him the history of our company, my background, etc., because I knew he could handle it and I knew how to be flexible within a structured conversation.

Would I use the exact same approach with a different person? No. Would the structured parts show up? Yes.

Here's a story that shows the need to know where we are in the conversation and to be flexible.

---

### When We Get Mad, We Still Must Remember Which Skill to Use

The president of a small naval ship supply company agreed with me to provide some sales training for his 15 sales people. As a final step, he wanted the chairman to meet me and sign off on our agreement.

After the introduction, I expected the president to describe the program. Much to my surprise, he said nothing, so I started the conversation with his chairman.

**Pete:** "John, I appreciate your time. *Attention* Would you like to ask some questions or have me make some comments?" *Benefit*

**John:** "You make some comments." *Resistance*

I started to describe the program and he picked up his financial report and started to read it. I could feel my face starting to turn red, so I did what I always do when people stop listening. I stopped talking.

He looked up and said, "Keep going!" *Resistance*

At this point I was irritated with him and the president. I knew I was going to blow the whole project if I didn't attract his attention. I needed to structure the conversation. I needed to start by getting his attention.

**Pete:** "John, you have a decision to make: put in this sales training or sell the company!" *Attention*

**John,** dropping the financial report: "What the hell do you mean?" *Resistance*

**Pete:** "John, you're in an industry that is shrinking.  *Attention*  The only way to make more money is to take market share away from the competitors.  *Benefit*  This sales training will do that."

**John:** "Tell me how you can do that." *Resistance*

A structured, flexible conversation allows for the other person's communication styles, no matter what they are.

---

Every responsible conversation requires that we switch back and forth between listening and speaking, in a flexible way, until both parties exchange sufficient information to come to an agreement.

It's easy—once we become skilled listeners and speakers. Those skills are the focus of the next two chapters.

# CHAPTER 5

# Responsible Listening: The Core Competency of a Leader

*L*eaders listen 45% of each day and 5% of them are trained to do it.

Robert Frost said, "Education is the ability to listen to almost anything without losing your temper or your self-confidence." Wow! A free translation is that we can't learn anything new without an ability to listen—and listen when under attack.

How can people *lead* if they cannot *learn*? Ninety-five percent of us don't learn anything new even in easy conversations. The reason? We've never learned the *skill* of listening. This inability to lead or ability to lead shows up most often when people are promoted from the head of a technical group to a general manager's position. Now they need to listen to people from disciplines they have not mastered.

> **Responsible Listening**
> I accept 100% responsibility for understanding, no matter how poorly the other person communicates.

Read the material in the following boxes to learn about what listening involves.

---

### Are You Part of the 5% Who Know the Fundamentals of Listening?

Often I start a listening workshop by asking, "Who is the best golfer in the room?" After a lot of laughter and finger pointing (obviously, whoever is the best golfer spends a lot of time on the golf course, not working), the best golfer surfaces. I bring that person up to the front of the room and ask about his or her handicap (the lower the score, the better the golfer). I ask, "How often do you play? How often do you practice?"

Then I ask the individual to describe to the group, in detail, the *fundamentals* of the golf swing. The individual immediately assumes the correct stance and without hesitation goes through the specific fundamentals, starting with placement of the feet and grip on the club and finishing with a demonstration of the swing.

When it is evident to everybody in the room how knowledgeable this individual is, I thank him or her and say, "I'd like to switch the conversation. It's evident you understand the fundamentals of a golf swing. I want you now to demonstrate something you do 45% of every day! Please describe to the audience, with the same detail, the fundamentals of listening. What do you do when listening?"

99% of the time a look of dismay and disbelief spreads across the face of the individual. The audience goes quiet. 95% of them know they could not give that demonstration, other than mentioning "making eye contact" and "nodding."

How would you answer the question if you were in the workshop? Why not briefly list below the fundamentals of listening that you have learned and practiced and that you use when you are listening 45% of your time each day?

#### Your Fundamentals of Listening

1.                                    3.

2.                                    4.

You can confirm your answer at the end of the chapter, where we summarize the fundamentals in a listening self-evaluation sheet.

---

---

## Listening Is Hard Work but the Payoff Can Be Dramatic

I was coaching an executive who was described to me as "the best troubleshooter we have but he kills off people in the process." This executive was so driven to get results he didn't listen at all to new information. He dictated what was to be done based on his years of experience.

We used a series of drills to teach him to listen. He had great difficulty doing them. After about a half-hour, he suddenly did a drill right.

I laughed and said, "You got it."

He laughed and said, "Yeah—but I'm sweating. This is hard work!"

---

Initially, learning to listen may be hard work, because we learned listening the "old-fashioned way," by not being listened to. We know what it feels like to be interrupted repeatedly in the middle of a sentence, to be told that children are to be seen and not heard, to respect authority. This lack of listening taught us the need to talk through, over, and around people so that we can be heard. It is not surprising that 65% of executives have been trained in speaking skills, while only 5% have taken a skill course in listening. Our business experience is "whoever draws the first breath is declared the listener."

However, the tide has turned. Global competition is forcing us into teams. Total Quality Management and cross-functional teams are the rage. Managers spend well over 50% of their time in meetings listening for new ideas, listening to make new changes. The problem is that few hear anything new or make new changes because they don't know how to listen.

Jon Katzenbach in *The Wisdom of Teams* says that high-performance teams are rare because, along with a high-performance standards, they require team members to have a "high degree of personal commitment to each other." A commitment to team members is difficult without an ability "to listen to almost anything without losing our temper or our self-confidence."

Possibly my initial realization that I didn't know how to listen will encourage your interest. Here's the story.

---

### When You Listen, What Are You Missing that You Don't Know You're Missing?

In 1972 I had been in psychotherapy for two years, twice a week, once a week individually, once in a group. One night I was reading to the group a serious letter from my father to me. Suddenly, all six people broke out laughing.

I was upset. I angrily confronted the guy sitting across the table from me. "What the hell is so funny?"

His reply, "Your father is weird." (Truth was he was far from weird. *We* were weird.)

But here's the point to the story—about the ability to listen. A thought flashed through my mind. If one of them laughs, I have a right to be mad. But all six are laughing. I must be missing something!

---

So the question is What are you missing in conversations? What are you missing in relationships, in information? How much less will you miss if you become a skilled, responsible listener?

We'll find out now as you learn and practice the skills of responsible listening.

## I Accept 100% Responsibility for Listening

A responsible listener is a person who accepts 100% responsibility for understanding what other people say, *no matter how poorly they communicate*. When we are willing to accept this responsibility, we can no longer get angry with the other person but must stay focused on helping the other person to speak in a clearer, specific way so we understand what he or she is saying.

Responsible listening is a special kind of listening. It can be an exhausting skill to use all the time, so we need to choose to use its fundamentals only when:

➤ we need accurate information to make an informed decision,
➤ we want to maintain or build a trusting relationship,
➤ we need to reduce the emotions of the other person.

Responsible Listening is not listening as we think of it. Responsible Listening is a special kind of listening. *It is the speaking we do before we respond.*

When we don't listen, our usual communication model is stimulus-response.

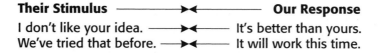

**Their Stimulus** ──────►◄────── **Our Response**
I don't like your idea. ──►◄── It's better than yours.
We've tried that before. ──►◄── It will work this time.

But responsible listening is the speaking we do before we respond.

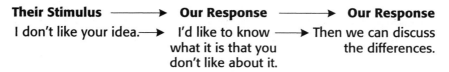

**Their Stimulus** ──────► **Our Response** ──────► **Our Response**
I don't like your idea.──► I'd like to know ──► Then we can discuss
what it is that you          the differences.
don't like about it.

Responsible listening is the speaking we do to prove to the other person that we understood what his or her total message said. It saves us from attacking or defending. It allows for no judgment of the other person's character. Its only function is the present, what the speaker meant at this moment, in this conversation. Listening is the suspension of judgments—until we gain new information.

Responsible listening requires changing habits. It requires practice. It may not be easy, but the results will be:
➤ Effective problem-solving conversations
➤ An increase in trusting relationships
➤ Improved productivity and motivational management
➤ Better meetings
➤ New ideas accepted

## Specify, Rationalize, and Depersonalize

We listen responsibly in three ways:

> **Specify**. We do not respond to generalities. We listen to help a conversation become specific so we can solve a problem.

> **Rationalize**. We do not respond to emotionally charged messages. We listen to understand the emotions so we can have a specific, rational conversation to solve a problem.

> **Depersonalize**. We do not respond to personal attack messages. We listen to reduce emotion over a longer period of time until the individual hears his or her own messages and chooses to calm down. Then we can problem solve.

| **Listen** |
| --- |
| • Specify |
| • Rationalize |
| • Depersonalize |

## Making My Conversation Specific Gives Me Control

Most of our responses to other people's messages are attacks, defenses, or justifications, because we respond to their opinions, not to specific facts. So as not to attack, defend, or justify, we need to make a conversation deal with specifics. When a conversation starts, we need to listen to people's messages to determine if they're *valid* or *invalid*.

| **Specify** |
| --- |
| • Invalid |
| • Valid |

A *valid* message is one that includes specific information we understand. An *invalid* message speaks in generalities and ambiguities. But the ultimate criterion for a valid message is not the specific information alone, but whether it is specific enough for us to be 100% responsible for understanding what each of us said.

Here's an example of an invalid statement (unspecific, no information):

"I'm *too busy* to see you now!"

We may not put our reaction into words, but at least we might be thinking, "So what? I'm busy too" or "He doesn't think I'm worth his time" or "She's just stalling so she won't have to make a decision."

These mental conversations are fantasy. We make up reasons to attack, defend, or justify.

"My time is just as important as yours."
"I'm busy myself. So what?"

Responding to an invalid message blocks communication. We need to listen so as to turn an invalid statement into a valid one, one we can understand.

Here is an example of a valid statement (specifics, times, dates, amounts):

"I'm too busy to see you now. I have three appointments this morning starting in fifteen minutes, and I need the time to plan for them."

When a person is specific, we usually do not need to attack, defend, or justify. We can accept his or her specifics or expand on them.

"OK, I'll check with you tomorrow morning at 9 a.m."
"Thanks for the specifics. When will you have time?"

Since our job is to be a responsible listener, we need to be able to quickly identify the difference between invalid and valid messages. For practice, make up your own scenarios for each of the four statements below. Put an "I" in front of any of the invalid statements. (You need more information.)

Example: __I__ "That's not how we work here."

1.___ "Your people had better get it together."
2.___ "I just get the runaround from your people."
3.___ "This is totally wrong."
4.___ "I have a much broader knowledge than you do."

Now that you have identified whether the statements are valid or invalid, by listening, how would you make the invalid ones valid? We need to make an acknowledgment statement, then ask a question.

For example, in response to #1—"Your people had better get it together"—we might respond, "I'd like my people to get it together. What are your suggestions?"

How would you respond to the invalid statements below? Use a statement and then a question.

Invalid Statement

2. "I just get the runaround from your people."
   Statement:
   Question:
3. "This is totally wrong."
   Statement:
   Question:
4. "I have a much broader knowledge than you do."
   Statement:
   Question:

Think back for a moment to a recent conversation with a superior, a peer, or a subordinate. What invalid, generalized statement did that person make that you responded to without making him or her be specific first? If you had to do it over again, what statement and then question would you have used?

| The Invalid Statement | Your Listening Response (*statement then question*) |
|---|---|
| 1. | Statement: |
| | Question: |
| 2. | Statement: |
| | Question: |

We all know that the motto for real estate sales people is "location, location, location." If there is a similar motto for a responsible listener, it is "specifics, specifics, specifics." When a conversation gets specific, we can problem solve. Until it is specific, we are dealing with our mental fantasy, not reality.

## Turn Emotional Conversations into Rational Ones

Emotions! What do we do with them in communications? In business we usually don't acknowledge them, but they're there—hidden, lurking below the scene, ready to explode with anger or shouts of joy.

| Listening |
|---|
| Rationalize |
| • Stated Emotions |
| • Unstated Emotions |

But to most people they are confusing! And how powerful! Robert Frost expressed their power when he said, "Education is the ability to listen to almost anything without losing our temper or our self-confidence."

---

### What Emotions Do You Hear?

To prove the point about how confusing emotions are and how we can't learn without listening to them, I demonstrate it in team-building workshops with this exercise.

I tell the participants, "I'm going to send you a message. I want you to listen to it, then write down the emotion you hear, nothing else, one word—the emotion you hear.

"Here's the message—'Listening needs to be a required course for all high school students'" (a message sent with a deep breath, a sad look on my face, and a low tone of voice).

Silence.

Then I suggest, "Some of you share with me what emotion you heard."

People respond—"disappointed," "sad," "frustrated," "I didn't hear any emotion."

After hearing five different responses, I say, "Wait a minute! What's wrong with all of you? I sent the same message and you all heard it differently. Why?"

---

We are all different people. We all have different experiences of emotions. Yet when we listen to others, we are sure we know what emotion was sent. In addition to our different experiences of emotions, we all have different motivations when we hear them. If we are action-oriented people, we may not even hear emotions. They have nothing to do with getting results. However, if we are idea-oriented people, we not only hear the emotions but also think about what was said and how and why—before we respond.

How we experienced the expression of emotions in our families affects how we handle them today. I grew up in a family with a strong grandmother who routinely and angrily insulted my father. My mother periodically sounded like her mother, particularly if my father was late for dinner. I learned how to avoid strong emotions, particularly anger.

Now, through the skills of responsible listening, I can respond to strong emotions. What I do is make them rational.

## Emotional Messages Need to Become Rational

We know that responsible listeners are 100% responsible to make invalid conversations (generalizations) into valid conversations (specific). What makes responsible listening even more difficult is that a responsible listener is 100% responsible to clarify emotional messages and help them become rational messages.

Why should that be difficult? It's difficult because:

➤ Emotional people send emotional messages.
➤ Unemotional people send unemotional messages.

That's difficult because both assume their way is the right way!

Here's a coaching story that highlights the different ways people hear and use emotions and why an essential listening skill is the ability to turn emotional messages into rational ones.

---

### Do You Yell at People? Of Course Not!
### But Some People Know You Do!

I started the third coaching session with an executive by asking this question, "What has happened in your communications since the last time we met?"

Her immediate response was "I had a strange reaction from a subordinate that I was having a meeting with. In the middle of the meeting she said to me, 'Why are you yelling at me?' I wasn't yelling at her. I don't understand her reaction."

Why should she understand? She does the same thing to senior managers. She was referred for leadership coaching because, when presenting in senior management meetings, she "raises her voice and talks faster." When and why does she do that? She does it when she perceives she is not getting the results she wants at the moment. She does it because she believes leaders need to be passionate about their beliefs.

To be a responsible listener requires skill practice, but first it requires knowing what you sound like. With this executive, we had audiotaped the previous session. I played back a segment of the tape where she cut me off, raised her voice, and talked faster because she was trying to make a point that I was having difficulty understanding. After hearing that segment, she knew what people were talking about!

Also, in response to her question about her subordinate, I explained to her, "What yelling is depends on our experience with yelling. My guess is your subordinate comes from a family or situations where it was considered inappropriate for people to raise their voices. In fact, it was discouraged and not allowed.

"Raising your voice literally may hurt her ears. Worse, it definitely shifts her attention from listening to the facts you are presenting to defending herself—'Why are you yelling at me?'"

Before we practice listening to clarify emotional messages and help them become rational, think for a moment: What is your reaction to people who raise their voices, who express strong emotions? List below two people who send emotional messages. How do their behavior and your reaction to it affect the sharing of information and your relationship?

| Name of Person | Emotion | Your Reaction |
|---|---|---|
| | *(anger, yelling, etc.)* | *(verbal and non-verbal)* |

1.

2.

Being aware of how you experience emotions is essential to developing your skill as a responsible listener. The next coaching

---

### Bullsh_t!

"Bullsh_t" is an ordinary word, depending on how it is used and by whom.

A senior executive requested communication coaching to ensure his eventual promotion to the presidency of his organization. He had been told he was "too aggressive."

He also is an executive who focuses on short-term results. It is a fact that many results-driven people like him rarely are bothered by aggressive people or conflicts. Conflict to them is anything slowing down the process of getting a result. It is people disagreeing with him in any conversation, people taking too long to explain themselves, or people wanting to review all the alternatives. Anything that slows down the process of making a decision is conflict and naturally requires aggressive action. Not surprisingly, he didn't think he was "too aggressive" and he hadn't asked anyone what he did that seemed "too aggressive."

I asked this executive to describe a recent conversation in which he got frustrated. In response, he described one conversation by saying, "Bullsh_t! We have to move ahead on this or we're going to get beat out by our competitor."

The word "bullsh_t" rolled out of his mouth without hesitation. It was just a natural part of the statement. It was part of his personality. He probably used it to get results.

I didn't draw his attention to it until we had spent sometime discussing how people are different from one another, how emotions affect them, how people listen to us. I even told him the story of a senior executive at a major bank who grew up in a family where his father wouldn't let anyone raise his or her voice. As a result, he never responds to an emotional or aggressive statement. He sits quietly until the upset person quiets down. Then he continues the conversation as if nothing had happened.

Finally we got to the point in the session where we talked about new communication strategies for him. I told him, "I have a new strategy for you—never use the word 'bullsh_t' again."

He looked at me, with a thoughtful face, and said, "Too aggressive, huh?"

story may help you put emotions in a personal perspective.

As I indicated earlier, Daniel Goleman in *Emotional Intelligence* states that we have two brains. One accumulates rational information and one is stored with old emotional responses. The way the body functions is that when strong emotions are stimulated, they may "short-circuit" our rational brain. We cannot access all the information we have stored up from years of experience. Therefore, we need to not let our emotions "short-circuit" our rational minds if people send us emotional messages. Conversely, if we send emotional messages, we need to be aware they may "short-circuit" our listener's ability to hear us.

## Identify the Difference Between Stated and Unstated Emotions

To be able to rationalize all messages, we need to identify the two ways people send emotions—stated or unstated.

A *stated* emotion is one that uses the emotional word in the sentence. For example:

➤ "I'm *angry* with you."
➤ "I *love* you."
➤ "I'm *depressed* at the moment."

An *unstated* emotion is one that is sent without the emotional word and has a good chance of being misinterpreted by the listener. For example:

➤ "Can't you see I'm busy?!" *(angry)*
➤ "I want to change my job!" *(depressed)*
➤ "You interrupted me again!" *(irritated)*

In this chapter we will practice listening responses to *stated* emotions only. *Unstated* emotions will be handled in the next chapter.

## Rationalize Stated Emotions

Suppose a person sent you this stated emotional message:

> "I'm *disappointed* with the way you treated me in the meeting."

| Listening |
| --- |
| Rationalize |
| • Stated Emotion |
| • Emotion Is the Message |

How would you respond? Would you respond with statements similar to these?

> "You weren't so great yourself." (*attack*)
> "I treated you the way you deserved." (*justification*)

None of these pass the test of being 100% responsible as a listener—to prove to the person you understand him or her. These responses are typical stimulus-response, with no listening. A listening response to an emotional message would be a statement, followed by a question, like this:

| Their Stimulus ⟶ | Our Listening ⟶ | Our Response |
| --- | --- | --- |
| I'm disappointed with the way you treated me at the meeting. | I don't want to disappoint you. | What did I do so I won't do it again? |

Our listening response to a stated emotion must include the emotional word the person used if we are to prove that we heard and we understand him or her, if we expect the person to listen to our response.

But why is rationalizing so important?

Because when someone sends an emotional word, that is the message. The person sending, "I'm *disappointed* with the way you treated me in the meeting" wants to know that *you know* how he or she felt. To respond without acknowledging the emotion is to:

> miss the point of the message
> prove you weren't listening

This coaching story may help those people who either

➤ shudder to think of reflecting back emotion
➤ don't believe reflecting back is necessary

---

### How Do You Handle Emotional People?

I was asked to coach a senior executive who had requested team building, because "my staff doesn't get along well." When I met with the human resource executive who was a member of his staff, she said, "We don't need team building. He needs to handle emotions. When we have disagreements in his staff meetings, he sits quietly, waits till we finish arguing, then continues the meeting as if nothing happened. So none of the personal disagreements get resolved."

**Bottom line**—a family history of never being allowed to express emotions, never being allowed to raise his voice.

**Strategy**—he would at least reflect back the word "concern." When his staff members argued, he would not use words like *mad*, *disappointed*, *angry*, *frustrated*. He would say, "I know you are concerned about _____. Let's explore the facts." That's the best he would ever do (he was age 52) without extensive training and advanced therapy. But it helped.

---

Here is a written exercise that may help you understand how to respond to stated emotions.

Below are three statements. They all state an emotional word. After each, we may want to practice our "listening" response. (Do not ask a question, but do make a statement.)

| Executive's Statement | Your Response |
|---|---|
| Example: "I'm damn *angry* that I have to write up another request." | "I'd be *angry* too if I had to waste time and energy doing that." |
| 1. I'm *surprised* they are calling to complain again. They're the ones who keep fouling it up." | _____ <br> _____ <br> _____ <br> _____ |

| Executive's Statement | Your Actual Response |
|---|---|
| 2. "I *admire* her as a manager. She's tough but fair and helpful." | _____ _____ _____ |
| 3. "It seems like a good idea … but I just don't know. I'm *afraid* some of my clients wouldn't like it." | _____ _____ _____ _____ |

When people know you have heard their emotions, they become more willing to deal with the facts, the specifics. When they do, we can get on with problem solving.

What is a new strategy for listening to another person? It's a two-step strategy: *Rationalize, then specify*:

➤ I listen first for any emotional words. If there is one, I must feed back that I heard it.
➤ If there are no emotional words, I listen for generalities. If there is one, I make the person become specific before I respond.

That's it—a two-step process: rationalize and specify.

Handling *unstated* emotions is a whole different opportunity. We discover that in the next chapter.

# CHAPTER 6

# Responsible Listening: Rationalize Unstated Emotions

*R*ationalizing unstated emotion is the hardest part of listening, but it is the pot of gold! It's where the wealth of information and the depth of relationships are.

> **Listening**
> Unstated
> Emotions
> • Guess
> • Confirm

Before we learn more about unstated emotions and their effect on how we listen, it may be useful for us to practice identifying the difference between the *stated* and *unstated* emotions we experience when listening to others. In the exercise on the next page, check (✔) once if a stated emotion is in the message and underline the emotion; check (✔✔) twice if an unstated emotion is sent and write a possible emotion at the end of the sentence.

Example:
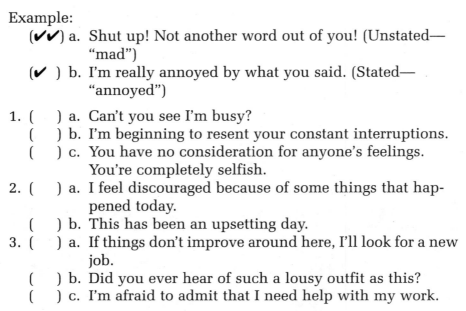
    (✔✔) a. Shut up! Not another word out of you! (Unstated—
               "mad")

    (✔ ) b. I'm really annoyed by what you said. (Stated—
               "annoyed")

1. (   ) a. Can't you see I'm busy?
   (   ) b. I'm beginning to resent your constant interruptions.
   (   ) c. You have no consideration for anyone's feelings.
           You're completely selfish.
2. (   ) a. I feel discouraged because of some things that hap-
           pened today.
   (   ) b. This has been an upsetting day.
3. (   ) a. If things don't improve around here, I'll look for a new
           job.
   (   ) b. Did you ever hear of such a lousy outfit as this?
   (   ) c. I'm afraid to admit that I need help with my work.

Now that we know the difference between stated and unstated emotions, we can work on unstated emotions and make them
specific.

A listening response to an unstated emotion *must* include a
two-step strategy:

**Step 1.** Reflect back your *best guess* of what emotion was sent.
**Step 2.** Then reflect back the confirmed emotion.

Here's what the conversation might sound like:
**Step 1.** "Don't talk to me like that again in a meeting." (unstated
        frustration)
        "I'll try not to talk like that, but why are you so angry?"
        (Your best guess)
**Step 2.** "I'm not angry. I'm frustrated that you interrupt me and I
        can't finish my sentences."
        "I didn't know I frustrated you. I'll try not to interrupt you
        so much. Now, I'd like to ...."

The reason it is a two-step process is because we hear an emotion from our own experiences and we may hear an emotional
message that is slightly different from the one the person sent.

This two-step process sounds simple, but people react differently to learning how to make unstated emotions rational. Below are examples of their initial responses:

➤ *Action-oriented person*—"Process takes too long, not necessary."

➤ *People-oriented person*—"It sounds like a confrontation. Can't do that. I want to share consensus."

➤ *Idea-oriented person*—"Emotions confuse the ideas and information. I'll explain rationally why I didn't interrupt her."

➤ *Structure-oriented person*—"Emotions disrupt a structured, critical approach. I dismiss them and continue the conversation as if no emotion was sent."

If any of these four different reactions is applied, none will demonstrate responsible listening.

They are the fantasies in our heads based on our personal motivations. The reality, however, is that the individual expects us to acknowledge the emotion we heard and understand his or her feelings. Until we do, the reality is that he or she *will not listen to our response*. Why should he or she listen? We didn't listen!

Here's a written exercise to let us practice rationalizing unstated emotions. Circle the answer (A, B, C, or D) that confirms the unstated feeling sent by the speaker. Then, in the answer you chose, underline the word you think describes the feeling stated. *Example*:

"There's one problem after another. What's the use?"

   A. Look, that's just the way it is.

   B. I'm surprised you feel that way.

   C. Tell me specifically what you're referring to.

   D. It's <u>frustrating</u> to keep running into problems.

1. "I worked so hard, and he screws it up!"

   A. Don't worry. I don't think you've really lost it.

   B. Are you sure you had the right groundwork established?

   C. We can't afford to have that happen. I'll straighten things out right away.

   D. When you put so much effort into doing well, it's pretty discouraging to see it jeopardized.

2. "Hey, I just got a letter congratulating us for doing good work."
   A. It feels great to be recognized.
   B. I know, but let's not let it make us complacent.
   C. Really? I'd better go read it.
   D. What did it say?
3. "I was depending on you to support my position. Instead, you
   let them tear me apart."
   A. I had good reasons for not speaking up.
   B. You're upset with the way I handled myself.
   C. I thought I did give you support several times.
   D. I was waiting for a signal from you.

The risk in identifying an unstated emotion is worth it. Depth
of relationships and quality of information require it. But if we
find it difficult to identify the emotion, we can always say, "I
know you're *concerned*."

## Depersonalize the Attacks and Defenses of People

"Depersonalize" doesn't seem like a word to
describe skilled listening, but that's exactly what a
skilled listener has to do to:

> **Listening**
> Depersonalize
> • Hypnotize
> • Spellbind
> • Fascinate

➤ calm down an irritated superior
➤ reduce pressures on an upset, disappointed subordinate
➤ refocus a disrupted cross-functional meeting
➤ keep a valuable client from deserting

Below are examples of successful executives. If they had mastered the art of listening, they might have been better leaders.

### To Execute Means to Perform, Inflict Capital Punishment; To Lead Means to Guide, Influence

Recently I had the privilege of conducting team-building sessions for
three presidents of significant business organizations. All three are
successful executives. All manage successful organizations. But how
much more effective their organizations might be if they were skilled

listeners! These scenarios surfaced during the team-building sessions:

The president of a major consumer products company described himself accurately in the middle of a team-building session: "If you bring it to me, I'll fix it!"

The president of the information systems division of a major communications company described his management style as follows: "We discuss a business issue. Then I expect you to carry it out. The last thing I want to do is monitor your progress."

The president of a banking service company requested coaching at the suggestion of his board of directors. In the middle of a team-building session, he said, "My job is to force you to perform. When I jump on you, I expect you to fight back, not disappear."

How do you depersonalize (listen to) the president of a company who is making strong, emotional statements to his subordinates in response to their feedback about his specific communication habits ("cutting them off in middle of sentences," "getting angry and insulting them")?

Here's how to depersonalize an upset president in the middle of a team-building session.

**President:** My job is to force you to perform. When I jump on you, I expect you to fight back!

**Me:** Wow, that's a strong statement. Do you really expect your staff to fight back against the president of their company?

**President:** Yes, I do. That's what they get paid to do. How can we get new ideas if people don't stand up for what they believe?

**Me:** It's evident to me you feel strongly about standing up for what you believe. You even look visibly upset about this matter.

**President:** I am upset. If they don't perform, we don't grow, then we all fail.

**Me:** So to keep them from failing, you see your job as forcing them to perform.

**President:** Right.

**Me:** That's one way to do it. You might be interested to know there are people in this room who will speak less and less, the more you yell and coerce.

**President:** Why would they do that? I'm trying to help them.

**Me:** You know you are trying to help, but they don't. Where in your history did you learn that your job was to help people by coercing them?

**President:** That's the way it was in our family. My father expected us to perform. He said it was his job to make sure we didn't fail.

**Me:** Clearly he did a good job of seeing you didn't fail. You are the president of a company at a young age. But let me ask some people in the audience a question. Now that you all know when he cuts you off, gets angry, and insults you, he is only trying to help you so you won't fail, who of you will fight back in the future when he coerces you?

**Staff:** Silence.

**Me:** Would someone tell him why you won't fight back even though you now know he's only trying to help?

**Staff:** "I couldn't do that." "I'm Scandinavian; we are taught never to get angry with people." "I never raise my voice." "I couldn't do that, particularly out of respect for authority." "I just couldn't do that."

**Me (to the president):** What do you think about that?

**President:** I'm amazed. That's a whole new way of looking at things. I don't know whether I'll be able to change that much.

As the president spoke and I listened (acknowledged, asked questions, identified stated and unstated emotions), people in the room were spellbound. They learned new information: the president was trying to be helpful, to keep them from failing. When he cuts them off in the middle of a sentence, when he gets angry and insults them, he thinks he's doing his job.

Understanding the president or anyone who is upset requires only two skills—specifying and rationalizing. In addition, it requires:

➤ That we give up our judgments of what the person is doing to us. It's fantasy, not reality. (The president was trying to be helpful.)

➤ The courage to stay in an uncomfortable conversation over a longer period of time. (Depersonalizing requires repeating the process of acknowledging and asking questions *three to five times*, in the same conversation—until we find the real reasons for the upset.)

Here is the process the president went through:

1. My job is to force you to perform.

2. We can't get new ideas if people won't stand up for what they believe.
3. If they don't perform, we all fail.
4. I'm trying to be helpful.

Why then is it so difficult to listen to upset people, particularly authority figures? All I have to do is acknowledge what they said, then ask questions, over a longer period of time. That sounds simple—except ...

---

### People Who Yell Attack Our Self-Esteem

At one time, I was working with two executives who reported to the same superior. Both had a hard time dealing with his emotional upsets. One executive said, "My boss is a screamer." I asked for an example. "The day before, in a fit of upset, he loudly proclaimed, 'Can't anyone in your department do anything right?'"

Anyone whose boss is a screamer knows what is it feels like to have his or her self-esteem attacked on a daily basis. It is emotionally draining and spiritually demotivating because tantrums (the things children do when they can't get their way) attack the four elements necessary to build our self-esteem:

➤ achieving the daily goals and objectives we set
➤ being cared for and valued by people *important to us*
➤ operating out of *our own* religious, moral, and ethical belief systems
➤ controlling the events and circumstances of *our lives*.

A boss's message like "Can't anyone in your department do anything right?" sent with strong emotions attacks our self-esteem in all four elements. Suddenly our priorities are changed, our feelings about our own lack of confidence may be heightened, our expectations of how people need to be treated with respect are shattered, and anxiety about the longevity of our job may increase. In one shout, the boss disrupts our day, and probably our subordinates' day, as we scurry around harassing them to overcome the perceived error.

Why is yelling ineffective? Because yelling makes the communication between us "unequal." Anytime someone misuses his or her knowledge ("I know more than you do"), power ("I'm the boss"), or strong emotions ("You've caused me a problem"), our self-esteem is under attack and the results are that we block, interrupt, or misunderstand the communication. It's not easy to hear clearly and be creative when we are under attack.

Our initial reaction to being yelled at is to protect ourselves, to justify what we did. However, if we are confident enough, in ourselves and in our boss, there may be a second reaction we might try to have. It is not easy, but we can mentally recognize at the moment she yells that *she* has a problem, not *us*.

"Can't anyone in your department do anything right?" sounds and feels like an attack, but it is actually her way of indicating her fright, disappointment, or upset over something happening to her. Like the president: he was afraid of failure. Whatever the reason, the individual has a problem he or she needs to get resolved and is going about it by communicating in an inappropriate, ineffective way—yelling.

So, we react negatively when someone attacks our self-esteem. The other reason it is difficult to listen to upset people is that their nonverbal communications also confuse the message. When the president of your company is in the process of intimidating you, it's hard to interpret it as "trying to be helpful." His nonverbals—tone of voice, face, gestures—certainly do not demonstrate that intention.

That's the bad news. The good news is much of the time the people giving off confusing nonverbal gestures are being critical of themselves. This coaching story may help you understand their self-criticism and make us more willing to depersonalize upset people.

## Do You Know People Whose Faces Turn Red? (Our Bodies Speak Our Mind)

I watched this 45-year-old executive's face and neck turn red, then return to normal, at least five or six times in our two-hour session. It was one of the reasons she was referred for communication coaching. People thought it demonstrated a lack of confidence.

It was obvious to her when it happened. She took off a light jacket a number of times because her body heat increased along with the blotches of red.

One of the facts about most nonverbal signs is that they are indicative of the internal mental conversations we are having while we are talking. If the conversations in our minds are the same as the words coming out of our mouths, they do not distract us. They make our words clear. If this executive had been saying to me, "I'm mad at you!" the red blotches would have been appropriate and emphasized to me the intensity of the feeling. In her case, she repeatedly told me her reactions had nothing to do with what I was saying.

I described to her another executive I had worked with who had smiled throughout a long discussion with her staff about her father's heart attack. Clearly her nonverbal (smile) had nothing to do with her verbal (words). I never mentioned it to her until I had videotaped a session. She was shocked to see the smile. She had never realized she did that. When we talked about her communications at home, I learned that both her parents were college professors. She was taught that she could get anything she wanted if she had a rational, logical argument. Unfortunately, while the thoughts she was having were a logical discussion about her father's heart attack, her fellow workers were dismayed at her smiling face.

I asked the executive with the red face if she could try to identify what she was thinking about when she started to feel the body heat. Best we could get was a mental conversation. She would be *criticizing herself*—"I should have known that." Also at work, she was *uncomfortable when she didn't know the answer.* "I should have known that."

That's not surprising, since she had spent most of her childhood being criticized by one parent to the degree that in communications she would defend herself by speaking faster. She also admitted figuring out in elementary school that if she answered quickly, she would not draw attention to herself by not knowing answers to questions.

The great value to practicing fundamentals of communications—speaking and listening—is they teach us to speak our mind clearly and not to have two conversations going on at the same time—one in our head and a different coming out of our mouths. When we speak our minds, smiles, and red faces disappear.

## Specifying, Rationalizing, Depersonalizing— and Robert Frost

Specifying, rationalizing, and depersonalizing are what Robert Frost calls education—"The ability to listen to almost anything without losing your temper or your self-confidence."

Responsible listening is the listening we do to prove to the other person we understand what he or she is saying. We use this skill when:

➤ We need a relationship with the person.
➤ We have information we need to share.
➤ The person is emotionally upset.

We only need the courage to use three basic techniques:

➤ Always acknowledge what the person said before we respond with any new information.
➤ Next, ask questions when we do not fully understand what was said.
➤ Stay in the conversation long enough to discover the reality of a person's upset or until we understand accurately what the person is saying.

Listening is a learnable skill. It is what we do 45% of each day—and only 5% of the people we work with have any idea of how to do it.

You are now part of the 5%. What is your action plan to develop further this essential skill?

One plan would include completing the responsible listening action plans that follow. Like any new skill, with practice new listening habits will grow and our ability to be responsible and to understand other people will build trust, gain new information— and keep our careers on a fast track.

## Responsible Listening: Practice Action Steps

Day 1:

1. Complete an action plan for the area of listening you want to develop.

2. Be an observer of communications. Listen to other people talking to observe their use of non-listening habits. (How often do they interrupt each other? What nonverbal signs are used? How often are they emotional?)

Day 2:

3.  Telephone calls that you initiate are appropriate times to practice. You can design cue cards to put next to the phone. Example—"Listen for tone of voice and feelings," "Make generalizations specific," "Guess at unstated emotions."

4.  Practice listening skills each day in the same routine situation, usually a no-risk situation—the store where you buy your coffee or newspaper or the first conversation with your secretary or assistant.

5.  Practice fundamentals while reading your mail. Select three letters. What emotions are stated or implied? Write your observations on the letter.

Day 3:

6.  Select one person and develop the depth of your relationship with this person by discovering more about him or her through use of listening skills.

Day 4:

7. Use the listening skills of responding to stated and unstated emotions with a family member or staff member. How did they work?

Day 5:
8.  Complete a "Rating of Ability" worksheet each Friday.

## Responsible Listening: Action Plan

**Subject:** State the specific area(s) or topics for improvement.

**Objective:** What do you want to accomplish? Your purpose? Broad objectives?

**Goals:** How will you know what you've accomplished? State specific targets or yardsticks by which you will measure change.

| **Problems:** | **Solutions:** |
|---|---|
| Barriers, obstacles, interruptions | Plans to avoid, deal with listed problems |
| 1. | 1. |
| 2. | 2. |
| 3. | 3. |

**Resources:** What people, time, equipment, materials, assistance are needed?

| **Activities** | **Time** |
|---|---|
| Sequence of steps required to bring about desired change | Use calendar dates, number of hours |
| 1. | 1. |
| 2. | 2. |
| 3. | 3. |

**Commitment:**

**Today's Date:**

# Responsible Listening: Rating Your Ability to Use the Fundamentals of Responsible Listening

For each fundamental listed below, place an "X" between 1 and 10 to rate your mastery of that fundamental (1 is the lowest, 10 is the highest). Repeat procedure in one week on _____ (Date).

### Mental Preparation

1. Accept 100% responsibility
   to understand                    1 ........................................... 10
2. Aware my mind runs faster
   than the other person talks       1 ........................................... 10
3. Listening is what happens
   between stimulus and
   response                          1 ........................................... 10
4. I do not lose my temper          1 ........................................... 10
5. I do not lose self-confidence    1 ........................................... 10

### Unequal Conversations

6. Anticipate emotional messages    1 ........................................... 10
7. Anticipate judgments of my
   character                         1 ........................................... 10
8. Anticipate solutions to my
   problems                          1 ........................................... 10
9. Anticipate justifications of
   behaviors                         1 ........................................... 10

### Specify, Rationalize, Depersonalize

10. Make general statements into
    specific ones                    1 ........................................... 10
11. Make emotional statements into
    rational ones                    1 ........................................... 10
12. Identify stated emotions
    (mad, glad, sad)                 1 ........................................... 10
13. Guess at unstated emotions
    (mad, glad, sad)                 1 ........................................... 10

**Fundamental Skills**

| | | |
|---|---|---|
| 14. Always use a statement first | 1 | 10 |
| 15. Ask questions only after a statement | 1 | 10 |
| 16. Always give back the stated emotional word | 1 | 10 |
| 17. Always guess at unstated emotional word | 1 | 10 |

# CHAPTER 7

# Responsible Speaking: How to Be Effective in a World of No Listeners

W hen corrected for misspelling a word, Mark Twain is purported to have said, "I can never trust anyone who can't spell each word at least two ways."

Unfortunately when we speak to people, there are two messages—the one we send and the one the listener hears. We don't trust the people *who don't* hear it the way we meant it. *They must be on their own agenda!*

> **Responsible Speaking**
> I accept 100% responsibility for people understanding what I say, no matter how poorly they listen.

The coaching story on the next page demonstrates how wide the gap can be between our speaking and the other person's listening.

## It's Sad—You Care So Much, Yet When You Speak, People Don't Trust You

We had been in our first coaching session almost three hours when I said to him, "It is sad that you care so much, yet people don't trust you."

I made that statement because he was sitting quietly, with his head down and tears noticeably in his eyes. What a visual and physical contrast to what I had witnessed and listened to up until then. Just before I made that statement, he had jumped out of his chair, grabbed me by my arm, and started to show me a Tai Chi movement we had discussed earlier. I'm an athlete, comfortable with men or women touching me; but his move was so quick and direct, I was startled. My physical space felt violated because he was so close. (Three feet is an acceptable distance; anything closer requires intimacy.)

I let him continue the demonstration for a few seconds. Then I stopped him and said, "That's what people mean when they say they don't trust you, that you tell senior management what to do, that they feel like you are waiting to pounce on them. I'm the consultant and you just took over the session."

He explained that he thought his demonstration was something I could use in a communication workshop (which it was), that he was trying to make a contribution to me because I had been helpful to him. He had realized I pulled back at first but he didn't stop because he wanted me to get all the information I needed.

We spent an amazing four hours together. He was an exceptional salesman. He helped build the division. He loved the company and the product and the clients, yet he had four new bosses in eight years and he worried about the business. He interrupted senior management because he cared for the company, and this new boss, in his estimation, was starting down his own path without sufficient information on clients and products. Besides the company issues, he was, by nature, a results-driven individual. He thought he never did things well enough. What senior managers were interpreting as rude and disrespectful behavior was his drive to overcome his inability to influence senior management to take the right steps, to be personally more effective.

It was when he realized this dichotomy that he sat in the chair, sadly, and said, "I don't want to be so intense. I want to slow down

> and not be so tough on myself and others." From that point on his progress was dramatic. He cared about people and his company. He was open to learning. He wanted results. He wanted to speak so people would listen.

This executive's motivations were worthy and he was speaking inappropriately. He needed help to speak in a responsible way, to accept 100% responsibility for people understanding him, no matter how poorly they listened.

## Bad News About Our Speaking

But even for skilled speakers, there is bad news. We speak in a world of no listeners.

**Bad News**
- 95% Unskilled
- 650-Word Gap
- 50% Prejudiced

There are three major reasons why we speak in a world of no listeners. Here are two of them:

1. 95% of the people we talk to are not skilled listeners. They have never read an article or book on listening. They have never taken a two-hour skill course in listening. They spend 45% of their day listening and have no idea how to do it yet think they do! All our well-chosen words fall on unskilled ears.
2. There is a 650-word gap between how fast we speak and how fast people hear. Physiologically, we can speak at a rate of 150 to 250 words a minute. Our listeners are capable of hearing up to 750-950 words a minute. They hear faster than we talk.

What do they do with the extra time? Think for a moment about the communication habits of a person with whom you communicate, at work or at home. He or she may engage in the nonverbal habits listed below. Check off ones you know he or she does when you are speaking:

❑ Allows emotional reactions to block hearing my message
❑ Thinks of questions to ask while I'm speaking
❑ Argues mentally
❑ Gives off body movement indicating impatience

❑ Projects doubts, hostilities, and prejudices by facial expressions

❑ Resists with increased emotional tone to control communication

Nonverbal signals are only part of the 650-word gap. There are verbal signals people give off as well. Which of the following verbal signals does this person send when you are speaking?

❑ Arrives at conclusions before I finish and interrupts me

❑ Defends his or her own point of view without considering what I said

❑ Asks questions about what he or she is interested in, not what I said

❑ Gives back irrelevant, burdensome information

❑ Speaks at the same time

As an experiment, you might want to go back over these lists of nonverbal and verbal signs of not listening and check the areas you know you do when the other person is speaking to you.

Here's the third reason why we speak in a world of no listeners:

3. People are poor listeners because they listen from their own motivational needs for *time and information*. For example, if our need is to speak long and give in-depth information and we are talking to someone who needs an immediate result and little information, that person will interrupt and cut us off. However, if we need to make quick decisions based on current information and we are talking to someone who believes he or she needs to give us a lot of information and take time to get that information, that person will stall decision making and inundate us with questions.

## Good News About Our Speaking

When we recognize that we are speaking in a world of no listeners, we can move ahead to the good news about speaking. There are fundamentals of responsible speaking that bridge the 650-word gap between what we say and what the listener hears.

**Good News**
- 2 Strategies
- 3 Fundamentals

These fundamentals start with a commitment to accept *100% responsibility for people understanding what we say, no matter how poorly they listen.* When we accept responsibility for how well people listen to us, we can no longer get angry or disappointed with them, but during conversations we must stay focused on improving the clarity or truthfulness of our speaking until the other person indicates understanding.

Part of that 100% commitment includes mastering two strategies and three essential fundamentals. The preliminary strategies require that:

➤ we focus the listener's ability to understand our message
➤ we minimize the listener's expenditure of energy while listening

### Strategy 1. Focus the Listener So He or She Understands Our Message

Many times we will start a conversation when the other person is doing something else or is distracted.

It is a waste of our time and energy to provide information *if people are not listening.* It is our responsibility to help them focus, not on what they have been thinking about or are doing but on what we will say.

Our responsibility is to eliminate any physical distractions, to get a commitment to the necessary time for a conversation, and to suggest a reason for the other person to pay attention. Here are three examples of focusing the other person before we start our real message.

➤ "Suzanne, you obviously are in the middle of a project." (She's typing on the computer). "Can you spare three minutes? I'm leaving town today and you asked for specific information."
➤ "Pat, we need to discuss this order. So as to save you time and energy, let's step into my office to avoid the noise. The discussion will take three to five minutes."
➤ "Bob, in relation to the decision we made yesterday, there is additional information you need before you implement it."

Reflect on two recent conversations you started when the other person wasn't really listening. If you had a chance to repeat the conversation, what would you say (time, physical distraction, reason to listen) to focus the listener *before* you start the real conversation?

1.

2.

What about the opposite situation, when people walk into our offices and start talking *before we have time to focus*? Here's a coaching story about the problems of focusing ourselves and others.

---

### Small Talk Is a Waste of Time!

As her secretary introduced me to her from the door, she got up, came over, shook my hand, walked back toward her desk, and—before she reached her seat—started talking with her back to me about what she wanted to get out of the meeting. By the time I was seated, she was into her third or fourth sentence about what she needed.

I let her talk a couple of sentences more and then said, "Good morning. How are you?"

She looked at me as if that was the dumbest statement she's ever heard. And from her viewpoint it was. The motivational style inventory she had completed before I met her told me her main motivation in life was to get results. She didn't want results just by the end of the day; she wanted them throughout the day, in every conversation, with the least amount of time spent!

The reason I was to coach her was because she treated everyone that way, including her boss and her subordinates. I told her that she might want to know that I hadn't even sat down before she was already telling me what she needed out of the meeting and, frankly, I missed what she said.

She said, "I know that happens, but I find small talk to be a waste of time."

---

She's right! With some people, small talk is a waste of time. For others, it's absolutely necessary to help people get focused.

Whether we call it small talk or focusing the listener, we need to accept responsibility to not start the conversation until both people are focused.

## Strategy 2. Minimize the Listener's Expenditure of Energy

The second strategy is to minimize the energy the other person expends when listening to us. Think back for a moment to the last conversation in which you had difficulty listening to someone speak to you. What did that person do? Here are three possibilities. Check any of the three the speaker did to you, then add your own at the bottom.

❑ Gave irrelevant information
❑ Gave too much information
❑ Raised his or her voice and talked down to me

Now add yours here:

❑
❑
❑

Most people burn up energy trying to understand difficult or unclear messages. Here are three speaking tips to minimize a listener's expenditure of energy:

**Tip 1.** Speak in short segments.
**Tip 2.** Provide only 30% of the information we know.
**Tip 3.** Use the listener's language (terminology, etc.).

### *Tip 1. Speak in Short Segments*

Why speak in short segments? Because there is the 650-word gap between how fast we can talk and how fast people can listen. If we provide voluminous information, our listeners' minds start to think about their own experiences and that distracts their attention from focusing on our message. Provide one or two ideas. Then stop talking until you get their reaction to them. Without hearing their comments, you have no idea what they're hearing.

### Tip 2. Provide Only 30% of the Information We Know

This coaching story gives an example of what happens to senior executives who get too much information.

---

## I Get Frustrated When My Staff Gives Me Too Much Information

I turned to the gentleman sitting next to me on the plane and asked him if he preferred to have time by himself or to talk.

"Depends on what we talk about," he said.

"How about communications on your job?"

He discovered I was a communication coach. I discovered he was a president of a power company.

"I get frustrated when my younger executives give me too much information in a meeting. I don't know whether they are trying to impress me or they just aren't good at communicating. All I want is the information I need! I stop listening or I will cut them off. What do I do about that?"

"It's a complicated question for complicated reasons," I answered. "Different people have different experiences with authority. Some young executives who talk to you and give too much information are *avoiding being punished*. Their experiences in school, family, and business may be 'if you give the wrong answer, you get punished.' A second group are people trying to *avoid conflict*. They have experienced that 'giving a wrong answer will cause an argument,' which is considered conflict. Conflict is something to be avoided at all costs.

"Both groups are providing you with all the information they know, with the hopes that you can select something that will answer your question without them being punished or drawn into conflict. The question is, what are you going to do about it? Possibly you might ask them to give you only essential information and you'll ask for more if you need it."

He didn't respond to my statement and the conversation ended. Probably *I gave him too much information*.

---

But his frustration is a uniform frustration expressed by senior executives. Young executives give too much information to senior executives for legitimate reasons—they believe information is important, it's their time to shine, they worry about decisions being made with insufficient information. Regardless, the key to responsible speaking is to give only 30% of what we know, the right 30%, the 30% the other person needs to make the decision. The person will ask for the other 70% if he or she needs it.

### Tip 3. Use the Listener's Language (Terminology, etc.)

The third way to minimize a listener's expenditure of energy is to use that person's language and not force him or her to use ours. I made this point in a workshop I was doing for a human resource conference.

---

## Who in This Room Knows Nothing About Football?

The response to my question, "Who in this room knows nothing about football?" was a loud statement from the back of the room by a woman: "I don't know anything about football."

Not only did she say this in a loud, urgent voice, but she said it by waving her hand so I wouldn't miss seeing her.

I asked her, "Why do you want to know anything about football?"

She said, "My son plays and I go to the game every Saturday." She was intently focused on listening to me. She wanted to learn about football.

I needed to seek a common ground, to start with something she knew, rather than burden her with terminology that she didn't know.

"OK, what's the one thing you know about football?"

With a big smile she said, "When they run under the goal post, it's a touchdown."

So the one thing she knew for sure was not actually true.

I said, "You're close. Actually the next time you go to the game, if you look 10 yards in front of the goal post, you will see an extra heavy white line. That line is called the goal line. When they cross that line, it's a touchdown, rather than when they run under the goal post."

At that point, I stopped the discussion to point out how disappointed she would have been if I started inundating her with technical language like quarterbacks, wide receivers, guards, and tackles.

If we want to minimize people's burning of energy, we need to start where they are, with language that they understand, and build from there.

---

Now that we have covered the two strategies necessary to help us be responsible for people listening to us—focus the listener so he or she understands our message and minimize the listener's expenditure of energy—we can move on to the four parts necessary to maintain a responsible conversation.

## Fundamentals: Four Structured Parts

Every conversation must be structured if we are to accept 100% responsibility for people understanding what we say. We must structure it to bridge the gap between reality and fantasy, the gap between how fast I talk (150-250 words per minute) and how fast others can listen (750-950 words per minute).

| **Structured** |
| --- |
| • Attention |
| • Benefit |
| • (Resistance) |
| • Agreement |

What follows is an overview of the four parts. After the overview we will review the three speaking parts, one at a time. The three speaking parts—attention, benefit, and agreement—are the elements of Responsible Speaking. The fourth part—resistance—we covered in Responsible Listening.

### Overview—A Structured Conversation

**Attention.** At the start of a conversation, we need to capture the individual's attention with an idea of personal interest about his or her job performance, and/or organizational or personal goals.

*"Why should I listen?"* That's what people immediately want to know. 90% of the time people decide in the first 10 seconds whether to listen or not. If it's not immediately important to them, people start to think about other things.

**Benefit.**  Once we have their attention, people continue to listen for reasons that affect  their organization, job performance, and personal goals. They listen for:

*"What's in it for me?"* We need to answer that question immediately, because 90% of the time a person is thinking of himself or herself, what he or she will gain or lose.

**(Resistance).** We can expect the listener to make statements, ask questions, or perform an action indicating he or she needs more information, does not understand, or is not ready yet to agree. The person wants to know:

*"Why do I have to decide now?"* 50% of our time needs to be spent answering questions/listening to the other person so they get what information they need to make a decision. We forget that only 5% of the listener's job relates to us/our needs.

**Agreement.** 100% of the time we need to ask a question, make a statement, or an action to conclude agreement. The reason is the listener is thinking:

*"How can I avoid making a commitment?"* 65% of acceptances come after the fifth attempt to gain agreement. People resist a final commitment a number of times until they are convinced it's a better choice to move ahead rather than delay.

## Sample Conversation

A sample conversation follows, demonstrating the three parts of Responsible Speaking used in every conversation in which we accept 100% responsibility for people understanding what we say. After reading this sample, we will discuss each speaking part, one at a time.

**Attention.** Capture attention with idea of personal interest to the listener, dealing directly with subject you want to discuss.

> "Pat, I'd like you to *consider the one or two people this year for whom you think our staged learning approach might increase their productivity.*"

**Benefits.** Give one or two reasons why the individual's organization, job performance, or personal goals will benefit.

> *"We provide a special niche for an executive to adopt new communication strategies in a short period of time.* We work primarily with senior executives, many of whom require increased sophistication in communications before they can move to the next level."

**Invite Participation/Agreement.** A question, action, or commitment used to get agreement or uncover hidden objections.

*Question:* "Can we talk about a specific executive you would like to have improve communications."

*Action:* "Let's put on our calendars a date to start your first individual."

*Commitment:* "My understanding is you are committed to starting your first executive within two weeks."

Before we move to Chapter 8, in which we'll practice the skills of *Responsible Speaking*, you may want to confirm your knowledge of *Attention, Benefits*, and *Agreement* by conducting the following steps:

1. When people call you on the phone, listen for their attention, benefits, and agreement.
2. Read recent mail you received, particularly advertisements. Can you identify benefits suggested to you?

# Speak Short in a World of No Listeners

## Practice the Three Parts of Responsible Speaking

### Part 1. Attention

We start each conversation with an attention-getting statement to capture the listener's mind so it won't run faster than we can talk. We have to start with a statement about his or her job, performance, or personal and/or organizational goals.

| Attention |
|---|
| • Their Job |
| • Their Performance |
| • Their Goals |

Sometimes it is easier to start practicing this fundamental in letters we write, because we have time to think about an appropriate beginning. Then we can move on to vocal conversations. Below are examples of the first lines of letters I recently sent. They may provide an insight into attention-getting statements:

Dear Pat,

   In September I wrote to a selected group of people to discover their interest in receiving a coaching story monthly. I'm not sure I sent you that letter, and *I want you to be part of this special group.*

Dear Tony,

   As always, *when you suddenly hear from a friend*, they'd like some help.

The attention-getting statement only serves to grab their interest long enough to make them want to read further in the letter or listen a few moments longer. Think about at least two letters you will write. How will you start them with an attention-getting statement, question, or action? Write those statements, questions, or actions in the spaces below. They will help you understand Part 1—Attention.

1.

2.

3.

Once we can use the attention-getting statement when writing letters, we need to put the fundamental into "live" conversations. Below I have listed three examples for different situations we all face on a routine basis. Under my example, write your own, based on your situation that will come up in the next few days or weeks.

1. My weekly staff meeting:  "Thanks for coming. This meeting is scheduled for one hour. We'll stop on time so you can meet your other scheduled obligations. *The objective to be reached before the meeting ends is ...*

Your staff meeting:

2. My conversation with a subordinate: "Joe, at the end of this conversation, I'd like to know the specific steps you will take to reach *your stated goal*."

Your conversation with a subordinate:

3. My conversation with my superior: "Jane, *the information you requested* is complete and it may take ten minutes of your time to hear it."

Your conversation with superior:

The *attention*-getting statement is direct and practical. It states the agenda for the conversation. It tells the listeners exactly what limits we'd like to set for the conversation and tells them how it applies to them.

Many people think this approach is too direct. They believe we need to provide needed information before we reveal the real reason for the conversation, to build a case for people accepting our request. The problem with being less direct is that:

➤ Our listeners fail to ever get focused: their minds run faster than we talk.
➤ Our listeners burn up energy trying to understand us: they don't know how to structure the information we give.

When people resist this direct approach, I ask them if they are good writers. Most people respond positively.

Then I ask them, "What does the first line of a paragraph do?"

Their response: "It tells you what the paragraph is about."

Bingo! If we know how to write, we know how to speak! The difference is that writing in the quiet of our office is easier than starting a face-to-face conversation the same way. So, as one of the infamous lines of stage and movie says, "Trust me; you'll like attention-getting statements."

Possibly you'll trust me more when you understand how the attention-getting statement is quickly followed by Part 2 of Responsible Speaking: benefits.

## Part 2. Benefits

Once we have trapped a listener's mind with an attention-getting statement, the easy part of the conversation is over. The hard part is getting people to continue to want to listen. They want to know immediately:

| **Benefits** |
| --- |
| • Gain |
| • Pain |
| • Personal |
| • Business |

➤ What will they gain from listening?

➤ How will their personal goals be met?

➤ How will their business goals be met?

Here's the hard part. The *details of what they have to do* will not convince them of anything.

What will convince them to do something is what they gain or lose from doing that thing.

This is a major switch in communications. We need to verbalize what they will get out of our request *before* we tell them the details of what has to be done. Start with the details and people immediately let their minds run to the 650-word gap. Their minds start asking the question we should answer with benefits:

➤ Why am I listening to these details?

➤ Where is this conversation going?

➤ What will I get out of this?

As we did with the attention-getting statement, we can use benefits—the things people gain—initially in letters, because then we have time to think. Below are two examples of letters. The first describes features, the details. Frankly, no one buys the details; people buy what they'll get out of it (benefits).

The first letter describes our leadership coaching. Would you be interested if you got this letter?

**Dear Cathy,**

**Our Leadership Coaching is provided in three sessions. The first is a half-day. This is followed by two additional sessions of two hours each.**

**In addition, we provide a ninety-page workbook, which includes practical drills and follow-up practice exercises.**

**We videotape the second session and audiotape the third session so people can follow up by themselves.**

Would you buy based on this information? Probably not. But if I provided the following letter, would you be more interested?

Dear Cathy,

    Responsible Communications welcomes an opportunity to provide Leadership Coaching for one of your executives. Our coaching is aimed at:

    "Maximizing their strengths and eliminating their communication roadblocks, which will save them time, energy, and relationships." What we do differently than other firms is we:

- accomplish practical, specific results in a short time frame
- custom design sessions for specific behavioral changes you expect
- expand an executive's understanding of all aspects of communication

Major impacts will occur in the essential areas of:

- selling ideas and concepts
- maximizing creative conflict resolution between staff members
- motivating individuals with difficult, differing communication styles
- planning and managing productive meetings, large and small

    Attached are the details of the format.

    I'll call to answer your questions about what specific benefits you'd like your executives to gain.

### Letters or E-mail: Written Benefits

Here's a suggestion. Pull out a few letters or e-mails you sent recently, if you have some copies around. Underline the benefits you suggested. If there weren't any, rewrite one of the letters or e-mails to include benefits. Sample benefits are listed below, some of the reasons people agree to what we ask:

- ➤ make money
- ➤ gain recognition
- ➤ increase flexibility
- ➤ save money
- ➤ gain security and/or peace of mind
- ➤ increase satisfaction or reliability
- ➤ save time and/or effort

➤ gain convenience
➤ increase status

They are the kind of things that need to be incorporated into your letters.

### Vocalizing Benefits

Once we know how to write benefits, we need to plan to use them in real conversations. Here's an example of the difference between vocalized features and vocalized benefits. I use this story in sales workshops when I'm graphically explaining the differences between features and benefits, a distinction every sales person in the world must master who wants to be a responsible speaker.

---

## Selling the Benefits of a Physical Examination

When I get to the right place in a sales workshop, I demonstrate how prospective customers would react differently to hearing features and benefits. Here's the story I tell:

"See this medical instrument I'm holding up. It has a light source on the end. It's thirty centimeters long. It's half an inch wide. It's inserted in the rectum."

After the gasps and moans, I usually ask, "Does anyone hear any benefits to this procedure?" Needless to say, none of these features are particularly interesting to them.

Then I switch to benefits.

"However, let me present this procedure from a benefit viewpoint."

At that point I start over again and say the following:

"This medical instrument I'm holding will save the life of most men over the age of 40. If anything is detected, minor surgery will save 50% of the people whose lives would be lost if they failed to have this procedure. As a result of this single procedure, the quality of lives and the lives of many men have been significantly affected and men live longer and are a lot happier. Please step into the medical examination room to save your life."

---

We laugh a lot but the point is made. People buy benefits, not features. If we want to be effective communicators, we need to be able to talk benefits so that people want to do what we request of them. What follows is a written exercise that might help you use benefits in your next conversation.

### *Practice Developing Benefits*

Listed below are some of the general motives (profit, convenience, fear, personal satisfaction, comfort, envy) for people accepting benefits. Under each category are a few examples of each benefit category. Next to each category, write a benefit statement that might apply to a person you will be talking to in the next few days.

**Profit**
- Money saved
- Cost-effective
- Increased productivity
- Return on investment

**Example**
John, you can possibly *save money* in your budget by modifying a job description.
1.

**Convenience**
- Ease of operation
- Ease of purchase
- Time saving

**Example**
Let's *make our life easier* by changing the software system.
2.

**Fear/Guarantees avoid the fear of**
- Loss
- Pain
- Trouble
- Hate
- Criticism

**Example**
I'd like to *avoid the continual criticism* from our salespeople, so we need to change the communication system.
3.

**Personal Satisfaction**
- Reputation
- Self-improvement
- Prestige
- New or latest design

4.

**Comfort**
- ➤ Pleasure                                      5.
- ➤ Health
- ➤ Cleanliness

**Envy**
- ➤ Getting acceptance                    6.
- ➤ Praise and consideration
- ➤ Power
- ➤ Strength
- ➤ Loyalty

## Part 3. Agreement

The third and last part of Responsible Speaking is agreement. A Responsible Speaker is 100% responsible for ensuring that each conversation ends with both people having a mutual understanding, which might be an agreement or an agreement to disagree.

> **Agreement**
> • Statement
> • Question
> • Action

The reason we place the responsibility for mutual understanding on the speaker is that communication research indicates that in 25% of conversations the speaker will initiate an agreement and 25% of the time the listener will initiate an agreement. But 50% of the time people complete conversations with no clear agreement as to the next step.

How many times have we left meetings with no clear direction for follow-up? How many times have we finished a conversation with someone who we are sure agreed to something we discussed and we are shocked to find later that he or she did something different or denied having agreed?

These misunderstandings can be significantly reduced when we ask for an agreement at the end of the conversation 100% of the time. We may not always get a clear agreement, because the other person declines, but when we leave, we will know there was no agreement—or there was one.

That sounds like a simple task. Just ask for an agreement. But it's not so easy for many of us. We know that if we don't ask we can't be rejected. Somehow we don't make a distinction between personal feelings of rejection and people disagreeing with our idea or concept.

I was continually amazed at the number of times trained sales people avoided "asking for the business" at the end of a sales call. When I was a sales training manager, we conducted a full-week workshop on making presentations to a buyer, including making the visuals. The last visual was designed to ask for agreement. I would then go out on sales calls. The sales person would make the presentation, get to the last visual—and never ask for agreement. He or she would come up with statements like:

➤ "What do you think?"
➤ "Any other questions?"
➤ "Well, that's the presentation."

We human beings hate to have someone say, "No," so we don't ask and we go away with no definite answer or "I'll call you next week." Maybe one reason is that by the time we are 18 years old we all hear "no" 180,000 times and "yes" only 50,000 times. We are programmed to say "no" or expect "no."

However, if we want to be Responsible Speakers, we need to accept 100% of the responsibility for asking for agreement at the end of the conversation.

## What Is an Agreement?

An agreement statement made by a speaker at the end of his or her speech or conversation invites a clear reaction from the listener (what is the next step?) or uncovers another resistance (indicates the need for more conversation).

Sample agreements may be a statement, a question, or an action. Examples:

**Statement:** "As a result of our conversations, it sounds to me you intend to implement this program."

**Question:** "When will you begin implementation of this program?"

**Action:** "Here is the draft of the announcement to implement the program. Please add or delete as you see fit."

Here's an opportunity to confirm how you use agreements. Think about conversations you've had in person or on the telephone over the last few days. Then write down the agreement you asked for—a statement, a question, or an action. If you didn't ask for one, write down the one you would use if you had a chance to replay that conversation.

1.
2.
3.

Now anticipate a telephone call or a conversation you may have in the next few days. What is the agreement you will ask for at the end of the conversation?

1.
2.
3.

## Summary: Responsible Speaking

We have completed the two preliminary strategies and the three speaking parts of a conversation. There is an action plan that follows, so you can practice and become more effective as a Responsible Speaker, someone who accepts 100% responsibility for other people understanding what you say, no matter how poorly they listen.

> **Speaking**
> • Action Steps
> • Action Plan
> • Rating of Ability
> • Planner

The action plans include four steps.

1. **Suggested Action Step.** This list of situations will provide opportunities to practice and develop your skill as speakers.
2. **Action Plan.** This action plan will help you focus on the one element that needs the most work. By initiating a specific plan, old habits will die and new ones will grow.
3. **Rating of Ability.** This provoking evaluation may be filled out

at the end of each week as a reminder of the principles of Responsible Speaking and how well you are doing with each.

4. **Planner for Every Conversation.** This planner highlights all the steps to plan a conversation. This will help continue to reconfirm the principles each time you use it before a conversation.

Remember: the bad news is that we speak in a world of no listeners, because:

➤ 95% of people have never taken a skill course in listening
➤ a 650-word gap exists between how slow we talk and how fast they listen
➤ 50% of people are prejudiced before we start the conversation

The good news is that we can use two strategies and three speaking elements.

The two strategies:

➤ Focus the listeners so they hear our message
➤ Minimize the listeners' expenditure of energy

The three speaking elements:

➤ Attention-getting statements
➤ Benefits
➤ Agreement

## Responsible Speaking: Suggested Action Steps

Day 1:

1. Complete a separate action plan for each fundamental of Responsible Speaking: openers, benefits, agreements.

Day 2:

2. Practice the fundamentals while reading your mail. Do they provide openers, benefits? What is their attempt to reach agreement: a statement, a question, an action?

3. When people call you on the telephone, listen for whether they will use openers or provide any benefits for you.

4. Observe how often you immediately respond negatively to requests and determine why you resisted—fear of change, cost, insufficient information, hidden personal reasons.

Day 3:

5.  Plan an "opener" for all conversations you know you will initiate:
    ➤ asking a staff member to come into your office
    ➤ making any phone calls, particularly to people outside the company
6.  Practice providing benefits in all written communications.
7.  Practice the fundamentals in non-threatening situations: in a supermarket, at a party, at a family meal, etc.

Day 4:

8. Use the Responsible Speaking planner daily to prepare for all important conversations.

9. Teach elements of Responsible Speaking to staff members, family members, and friends. (You'll need an opener to focus their interest.)

Day 5:

10. Complete a Rating of Ability worksheet each Friday to track progress.

# Responsible Speaking: Action Plan

**Subject:** State the specific area(s) or topics for improvement.

**Objective:** What do you want to accomplish? Your purpose? What the other person will agree to?

**Goals:** How will you know what you've accomplished? State specific targets or yardsticks by which you will measure change.

| **Problems:** Barriers, obstacles, interruptions | **Solutions:** Plans to avoid or deal with listed problems |
|---|---|
| 1. | 1. |
| 2. | 2. |
| 3. | 3. |
| 4. | 4. |

**Resources:** What people, time, equipment, materials, assistance are needed?

| **Activities** Sequence of steps required to bring about desired change | **Time** Use calendar dates or number of hours |
|---|---|
| 1. | 1. |
| 2. | 2. |
| 3. | 3. |
| 4. | 4. |

**Commitment:**

**Today's Date:**

## Responsible Listening: Rating Your Ability to Use the Fundamentals of Responsible Listening

For each fundamental listed below, place an "X" between 1 and 10 to rate your mastery of that fundamental (1 is the lowest, 10 is the highest). Repeat procedure in one week on _____ (Date).

**Mental Preparation**

1. Anticipate that 95% of people are untrained listeners        1 .............................................. 10
2. Remember 650-word gap between speaking and listening   1 .............................................. 10
3. Anticipate differences between time and information       1 .............................................. 10

**Minimize Listener's Expenditure of Energy**

4. Speak in short segments        1 .............................................. 10
5. Provide only necessary information (30%)       1 .............................................. 10
6. Use listener's language (his or her terminology)       1 .............................................. 10
7. Provide information at listener's ability to absorb       1 .............................................. 10

**Attention-Getting Statement**

8. Make a statement about his or her job or performance       1 .............................................. 10
9. Make a statement about his or her personal goals       1 .............................................. 10

**Benefits, Not Features**

10. Use benefits in letters        1 .............................................. 10
11. Use benefits in telephone calls   1 .............................................. 10
12. Use benefits in face-to-face communications       1 .............................................. 10

**Agreements**

13. Accept 100% responsibility to
    get agreement     1 ......................................... 10
14. Use questions to get agreement     1 ......................................... 10
15. Ask for an action to get
    agreement     1 ......................................... 10

## Responsible Speaking: Planner for Every Conversation

***Person Contacted*** (Name and Title):

***Objective of this call*** (This is defined by the other person's action. What action do you want him or her to take, not what you will do?:

***Opener*** (Start with item of personal interest relating to listener's goals, responsibilities—pain or gain):

***Benefits*** (Reasons to agree, his or her needs or wants, business or personal, exist in listener's listening only):
List the features first, then translate each into a benefit.

| *Feature* | *Benefit* |
|---|---|
| 1. | |
| 2. | |
| 3. | |

***Resistance Expected*** (Can you anticipate his or her statement, question, hidden commitment?):

***Agreement*** (Question, action, statement, to get agreement):

CHAPTER 9

# Coaching People for High Performance— Theirs and Ours

*C*oaching people for high performance is part of the four S's in the Responsible Communications process. Before we launch into how to coach, a quick review of the whole process will provide a better understanding of where coaching fits.

The four S's are:

1. *Strategy*    3. *Skills*
2. *Structure*   4. *System*

As noted earlier, Peter Senge in *The Fifth Discipline* states, "A leader needs a communication system, which is what makes visible our limiting structure." Without a communication system, we revert to old habits, we communicate the old-fashioned way, we "wing it." Instead of "winging it," we suggest that there is a system, which looks like this:

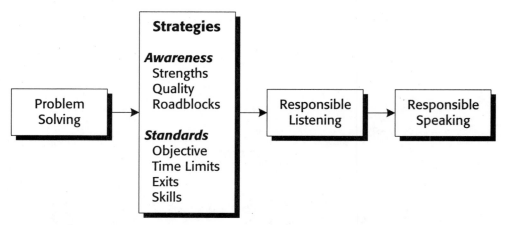

Before we start any conversation, we need to develop *strategies* for each conversation. We need to:

➤ be aware of our strengths
➤ recognize the quality of a conversation as being "equal or unequal"
➤ recognize that people block communication when they defend, attack, or justify their behaviors.

Once we are aware, we need to apply *standards* to each conversation:

➤ Have a clear *objective*—what do we want to agree to at the end of the conversation?
➤ Set a *time limit*—the length of the conversation to which we both are committed.
➤ Have techniques to *exit* difficult conversations that we don't choose to stay in.
➤ Apply the *skills* of Responsible Listening and Speaking throughout.

A basic, rational problem-solving conversation requires that we use two sets of skills—Responsible Listening and Responsible Speaking, as shown in the figure on the next page.

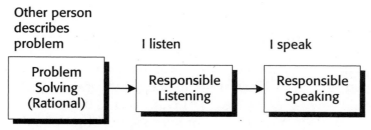

That system would be sufficient if all conversations were sent in a rational tone, when people can share information and build relationships.

Unfortunately, when other people get emotional, we may need an additional skill, called "Coaching." Coaching is helping other people solve their own problems.

Also, when we get emotional, we need to speak in a way such that the other person will be willing to help us solve our problems. That skill we call "Declaring."

Now, if we are going to be 100% responsible for the results of our communications, we need a system of four sets of skills:

➤ Responsible Listening
➤ Responsible Speaking
➤ Coaching
➤ Declaring

The process of the four S's now looks like this:

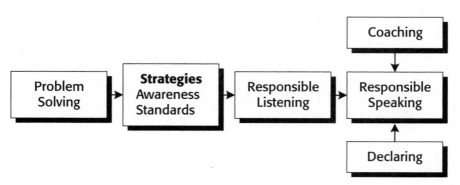

The process is three to one—three speaking skills to one listening skill. We covered Responsible Speaking in the last chapter. The two speaking skills of Coaching and Declaring we will cover now, to complete the Responsible Communication system.

## Coaching

One of the greatest opportunities for increasing productivity is to allow people to solve their own problems, to be creative within their own responsibilities. Too often supervisors are quick to say, "Do it this way" or "Here's what I want you to do" or "If you can't do it, I will." When we are too quick to solve other people's problems, two things happen:

➤ They don't learn to be responsible for their own problems.
➤ We spend time solving their problems, time that could be better spent expanding our own responsibilities.

Two coaching stories follow. The first demonstrates coaching another person to think through the options from which he or she can choose. The second demonstrates avoiding involvement so the other person is forced to determine his or her own solution.

---

### People Laugh and Have Fun When They Solve Their Own Problems

She was laughing and having fun when she said, "He'll go bananas when I start his lawn mower." But a few moments before, with great intensity and no sense of humor, she had said, "I need my husband to trim the lawn better. Compared to our neighbor's lawns, ours is a mess! He never completes the job and, when I tell him I think he should, his reaction is it's no big deal—but he never finishes the job right!"

Of course most of her life she had lived with a mother who couldn't stand for anything that was not in exactly the right place and done on time. If this executive had anything out of order in her room, her mother would severely criticize her.

This executive's need to avoid criticism shows up in her business life today. She never speaks up in meetings when she hasn't had time to be totally prepared or thinks she'll be criticized. Peers and superiors wonder why she doesn't share what she knows. Their perception is that she holds back information, but when she does speak up, it often is demanding and critical of others because they haven't done their work right and on time.

We worked on the issue about her husband not trimming the

lawn because reducing her need to criticize might free her up to speak more in corporate meetings and be less critical.

I told her, "We always have a choice when we communicate—and in our actions. For example, rather than saying to your husband, 'I need you to complete trimming the lawn,' what others choices do you have—choices that will force him to focus and possibly change his behavior?"

"I could say to him, 'I wonder what our neighbors think.'"

"What would his response be?"

"He'd say, 'It's not a big deal.'"

"OK, your statement wouldn't work because it has no pain or gain for him. He obviously doesn't worry about the neighbors; he hasn't completed trimming the lawn for years. What could you say or do that would attract his attention?"

She started to laugh. "I could start up his lawn mower. He'd go bananas, because he takes such good care of it."

"Do you know how to start a lawn mower?"

With increasing laughter, she said, "No, but I can learn."

"Obviously you are having fun with this idea," I said. "Why?"

"Because I can picture him racing around the side of the house and then panicking to see me using his lawn mower."

"What do you think he'll do?"

She laughed again and said, "I think he'll start to trim the lawn better when I tell him why I'm using the lawn mower."

Coaching is helping people to recognize they have choices. Most of us respond from our old experiences, designed to defend ourselves. But freedom and fun are possible if we choose to say things the other person will hear as a personal pain or gain, such as "I'm going to trim the lawn with your lawn mower."

This second coaching story demonstrates how, when we avoid becoming involved in someone else's problem, that person is forced to figure it out for himself or herself.

## Dad, Dad, You Have to Drive Me to Basketball Practice

One night my 12-year-old son burst through the front door at five minutes to six saying, "Dad, dad. You have to drive me to basketball practice or I'll be late."

Now basketball practice was at the local elementary school, about a ten-minute run from our house. Knowing he could get there safely, although a few minutes late, I responded, "I can't take you, you'll have to find another way."

"I'll be late," he said. "The coach will be mad."

"The coach may be mad," I replied, "but I can't go."

"Dad, I don't want to be late. He'll put me on the second team!"

"I hope he doesn't put you on the second team," I told him. "But I can't go."

He stared at me, thought for a second or two, then turned and started running toward the elementary school. He solved his problem—and I didn't get mad at him or have to go out!

I had choices. One would have been to say, "OK, jump in the car," and drive him to school. I also could have lectured him: "You are always late. I'll drive you, but this is the last time."

But coaching is about getting other people to making decisions to solve their own problems. We coach them sometimes by not getting involved in the process.

## Do's and Don'ts of Coaching

The fundamentals of coaching are easy. But doing them takes some practice. Here are the do's and don'ts. They involve primarily using Responsible Listening skills in a special way to help the subordinate perform in the future.

| Don't | Do |
|---|---|
| Give our solutions to their problems | Restate key points |
| Be critical of their solutions | Check the understanding |
| Ask our "agenda" questions | Ask clarifying questions |

# Critic, Player, Coach

But to use these fundamentals we need to make distinctions among the roles of critic, player, and coach.

## Critic

Anybody can be a critic. A critic is someone who tells us what we should have done. The Sunday papers are full of critics—art critics, sports critics, theater critics, financial critics. They give their opinions about what they think others should have done.

| **Critic (Past)** |
| --- |
| Judgments |
| Criticisms |
| Opinions |
| Bias |

Unfortunately, business supervisors easily slip into the role of critic. One reason people keep coming to supervisors for help to solve their problems is that, in the past, when they solved problems themselves, they were strongly criticized for their decisions.

> ➤"That was a dumb decision. Why in the world would you do that?"
> ➤"If you had come to me, we wouldn't have lost the client."
> ➤"Don't ever make a mistake like that again."

## Player

The people we supervise are like individual athletes, individual musicians in an orchestra. Once the game starts, once the music starts, they are on their own!

| **Player (Present)** |
| --- |
| Action |
| Results |

They have to perform, at the moment, in the appropriate manner. If they have been given practical and inspirational coaching, their choices of performing effectively are increased. If they have been criticized and are afraid of making a mistake, they will not perform to the expected level. Our jobs as supervisors are to turn loose a talented employee to use his or her God-given talents, to act, to get results—at the moment required.

## Coach

Thus a coach's job is to prepare people to perform in the future, to help them become more confident in their preparation and their abilities to solve problems when under fire, at the moment they are confronted with problems or opportunities or decisions,

| **Coach (Future)** |
| --- |
| Vision |
| Possibilities |
| Potential |

when the supervisor is not around. Criticism doesn't develop people. Coaching does!

## Coaching Is a Two-Step Process

The most important part of a coaching process is to decide to coach or not. Coaching is not appropriate in an emergency, when the cost is too high to justify time, money, and energy, and when the employ-

> **Coaching**
> Their Problems
> Coaching Skills

ees don't have the ability and resources to solve the problem. Coaching is appropriate under other conditions.

### Step 1. To Coach or Not to Coach

Coaching is appropriate in a particular situation. It is appropriate when the employee:

➤ is more emotional than we are
➤ has a problem whose solution will have a material effect (psychological or physical) on him or her
➤ has the resources to solve the problem
➤ does not have the "last word," but we do

Let's start with the "last word." In a coaching situation, the coach never has to get upset, talk to people in an "unequal" way ("I'm smarter" or "I have the power"), or dictate a solution. The supervisor always has the last word.

For example, when my son wanted me to drive him to basketball practice, I had the "last word." He couldn't force me to drive him. In business, if the supervisor controls the finances, he or she always can say, "We will not do that." If a subordinate wants to fire a member of his or her staff, the supervisor can always say, "No."

The first step, then, for a coach is to decide whether or not he or she has the last word. If he or she does and chooses to coach, then the other criteria dictate a coaching session:

➤ The other person is more emotional than I am.
➤ The solution will impact psychologically and physically on the other person.

➤ The other person has the resources to solve the problem.

Here are a few business situations in which we need to decide whether to coach or not. For each of the criteria listed, check "Yes" if it is a coaching situation and "No" if not.

1. A subordinate comes into your office unannounced.
   "I can't stand the way Mary talks to me. You have to do something about this." (upset)
   ____ Yes ____ No

2. Your supervisor comes into your office.
   "I'm having difficulty with one of my teenage kids. You seem to be good with your kids. I need your help." (frightened).
   ____ Yes ____ No

|  | Question 1 | | Question 2 | |
|---|---|---|---|---|
| What criteria did you use to decide? | Yes | No | Yes | No |
| more emotional than me | ____ | ____ | ____ | ____ |
| solution impacts on him or her | ____ | ____ | ____ | ____ |
| resources to solve it | ____ | ____ | ____ | ____ |

Here are two situations. Based on the same criteria, check if they are coaching situations or not.

1. A subordinate comes into your office unannounced
   "I can't stand the way Mary talks to me. I'm going to fire her today." (angry)
   ____ Yes ____ No

2. Your superior comes into your office when you are about to leave for an important meeting.
   "I'm having difficulty with one of my teenage kids. I need your help now." (demanding)
   ____ Yes ____ No

The answers to the questions above depend on the criteria you used to decide in these two situations. Remember, in scheduled conversations it's easy to decide whether to coach or not. In unscheduled ones it depends on the depth of the relationship, the urgency of time, and the magnitude of personal or business situations. But the criteria to determine whether or not to coach are the same.

## Step 2. Coaching Skills

We need to decide within minutes of the beginning of a conversation whether we will coach or not. If we decide to coach, we need to help the individual solve his or her problem without imposing our solutions. We need to:

| Coaching Skills |
| --- |
| Safe |
| No Specific Solution |
| Confirming Statements |
| Open-Ended Questions |
| Shared Solutions |

➤ provide a safe communication environment in which the person considers alternatives
➤ acknowledge we do not have a specific solution
➤ make confirming, thought-provoking statements
➤ ask questions so the person can think creatively
➤ share our alternative suggestions so the person gains a wider perspective

The story that follows demonstrates some of these coaching points.

---

### What Do I Do with a Peer Who Withholds Information in Our Meetings?

I was having lunch with a client executive when he asked that question. The purpose of the lunch was to demonstrate to him how we make judgments about people without sufficient information. In making judgments of others, we excuse ourselves from any responsible action and are content to assume there is something wrong with the other person.

I asked him how he knew the other person was withholding information.

"Because in our staff meetings with our superior, he is constantly giving information, but when we have a peer meeting without our boss, he contributes nothing."

"Maybe his actions have nothing to do with giving information," I responded, "but relate to his concept of authority."

"What do you mean?"

"Before I tell you what I mean," I said, "I want to ask you a question. Does he provide information to his subordinates?"

"Yes, in fact he dominates them with information and tells them what to do."

"Then my answer to you about authority is that when the boss is in the room, he knows who the authority is. When he is the boss, talking to his subordinates, he knows he is the authority. When he is in the room only with his peers, he doesn't know who the authority is, so he remains quiet. That's my guess why he is withholding information.

"The real question," I continued, "is what actions can you take to get the information you want, rather than be irritated because you think he is withholding it?"

"I can ask him in the meeting for specific information I think he has that I need."

"That's one action," I replied. "What's another?"

"I could meet with him separately and ask him to give me information I need."

"Good," I said. "What's a third choice you could make?"

"I could tell him I'm disappointed when he doesn't speak up because he could add a lot or even ask him why he doesn't speak up."

"Any of those are responsible actions you can take," I commented. "I have no idea what his response will be, but whatever it is, it will be more informative than for you to have a mental fantasy that he's withholding information in meetings."

Here are the five coaching steps demonstrated in the story.

1. *Provide a safe environment.* A safe environment has two elements, privacy and time. Coaching needs to be done in private. Once privacy is ensured, the two of you need to agree on a committed length of time. People will have a difficult time sharing intimate details and being creative if they feel rushed. Don't start a coaching session if the necessary time is not available.  Schedule for a later time or suggest, "I have ten minutes now. If we are not finished by then, let's set a date to finish the discussion. OK?"

2. *Acknowledge we do not have a specific solution.* The hardest part of coaching is to bite our tongue and keep our mouth closed when we know what they should do. The key to coaching is helping the person figure out his or her own solutions, not implement ours. "John, I'm glad to help think through

your questions and possibly come up with alternative answers."

3. *Make clarifying, thought-provoking statements.* My statement, "Maybe his actions have nothing to do with giving information but relate to his concept of authority," was a guess based on experience, not any fact. But it opened up the conversation to a new line of thinking. If he had said, "I don't think so," I would have needed to drop that line of thinking and try a different approach. Coaching is to use our experiences to provoke additional thoughts, not to force the process into our solution, our agenda!

4. *Ask creative questions.* "Does he provide information to his subordinates?" Open up an important fact—the peer doesn't withhold information with subordinates, which is the direct opposite of what he does with his superior. Now the conversation shifted from being about withholding information to the possibility the peer's actions were about authority. The key to coaching is to be open to the conversation going in a completely different direction—if we are willing to let it!

5. *Share our alternative solutions.* Once we are both clear that maybe the peer is responding to authority issues, not withholding information, we could move on to what the client will do to get the information he wants from the subordinate. Providing people with the opportunity to make a choice among alternatives is the key to successful coaching. For example, "What actions can you take to get the information you want, rather than be irritated because you think he is withholding it?"

Coaching gets to be fun when we can provoke creative thinking, not provide definitive solutions. As a coach, I need to keep constantly in mind the individual has to carry out his or her solution next time when under pressure and I'm not there.

Successful coaching provides alternatives to be selected by the other person, alternatives appropriate for them, at the appropriate time.

## Coaching Practice Drill

Now that we know the skills of an effective coach, we need to put them into practice. Here's a drill to use.

### Objective

Be alert for a friend or subordinate who seeks you out or seems upset. Use the following approach:

1. The coach's job is to help the person discover new insights leading to his or her solution. The coach does so by using these Don'ts and Do's:

| **Don't** | **Do** |
| --- | --- |
| Have insufficient time | Provide a safe environment |
| Give any direct solutions | Acknowledge that you do not have a solution |
| Make any judgments about the person | Make clarifying statements |
| Ask questions that force the person to defend a point of view | Ask creative questions |
| | Share your alternatives |

2. After the coaching practice, ask yourself these questions:

   ➤ Did I give the person my solution to the problems? Or did he or she solve the problem with his or her own solution or a new solution?

   ➤ Was I patient, allowing the person time to think and respond? Or did I press him or her for my quick, relevant solutions?

   ➤ How would I coach differently next time?

## Moving On

Now that we know how to coach people who have problems, we need to move on to the last speaking skill, Declaring. Declaring is used when we have a problem: we want someone to stop doing something he or she is doing or to start doing something he or she is not doing.

# CHAPTER 10

# Making Declarations So People Stay on Their Side of the Line

*D*eclarative speaking is used instead of *nagging*, *griping*, *attacking*, *defending*, or *justifying*. We use it when we need to draw a line in the sand. It says to the other person, "You have violated my physical and/or psychological space. Get back on your side of the line."

Declaring, the most difficult skill to perform, is the last in the system of Responsible Communications:

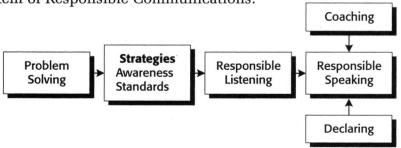

## Who Are Declarative Speakers?

Declarative speakers are people who accept responsibility for speaking in such a way that other people will choose to modify their behavior. Simply put, declarative speakers communicate so other people:

➤ will start doing what they are not doing
➤ will stop doing what they are doing

To be a declarative speaker, you must learn and use the fundamentals *at the appropriate time and in the appropriate situation*. Declarative speaking protects our physical and psychological space while continuing to respect the other person. Three declarative skills are declaration, straight talk, and emotional stand.

### Declaration, Straight Talk, and Emotional Stand

These three skills are used in the following circumstances.

| **Skills** |
| --- |
| Declaration |
| Straight Talk |
| Emotional Stand |

#### *Physical Space*

Someone is using our phone when we are expecting an important phone call.

➤ Declaration: "*I need my phone now.*"
➤ Straight Talk: "I need my phone now because *I'm expecting a scheduled call.*"
➤ Emotional Stand: "When you are talking on my phone so I can't get a scheduled call, *I get mad* because I can't keep my promise to the person calling."

#### *Psychological Space*

An emotional supervisor wants to fire one of our subordinates for reasons we don't agree with or don't understand.

➤ Declaration: "*I cannot fire Jane today.*"
➤ Straight Talk: "I cannot fire Jane today because *I need to review the facts.*"

➤ Emotional Stand: "When you ask me to fire Jane today, *I feel violated* because I have not had time to review the facts."

Each of these skills is used in different situations. To understand their use, you'll need to have in mind recent conversations in which:

➤ you were emotional about some act or statement
➤ someone asked or ordered you to do something that you were not willing to do

## Personal and Business Situations

We can make these skills relevant to our own personal and/or business situations in which people interfere with our lives (trespassing on our space, restricting our freedom, intruding on our feelings, hampering us from getting what we want, etc.). Next to each situation below, write the feelings you felt at that time. Finally, list the material effect on you in terms of money, time, and/or work.

Here are two examples:

Now give three examples of your own:

| Situation | Feeling | Effect |
|---|---|---|
| *Examples* | | |
| Someone using your phone when you need it | Mad | Blocks you from a commitment |
| Supervisor asks you to fire one of your subordinates | Violated | Expects a decision when you don't have sufficient facts |

1.

2.

3.

As you keep in mind the situations you've listed, we'll review both of the situations mentioned earlier, in the light of the three skills of declaring:

➤ Declaration
➤ Straight talk
➤ Emotional stands

## Declarations

Here are the two examples of declarative statements given earlier:

➤ "I need my phone now."
➤ "I cannot fire Jane today."

Each declarative statement demonstrates the basic fundamentals of all three skills:

➤ Repeat the same statement a number of times.
➤ Make no accusations about the other person ("You" messages).
➤ Make only statements about what you will or will not do ("I" messages).

Here's a demonstration of the first. A friend is standing in your office using your phone:

**You:** I need my phone now.
**Friend:** I'll be done in a minute.
**You:** I need the phone now.
**Friend:** I'm almost finished with my conversation!
**You:** I need the phone now.

We deliver this message in the same firm tone of voice. We do not raise our voice or get impatient. We deliver the message in a firm, factual, and deliberate tone of voice, repeatedly.

Here's the second demonstration.

**Supervisor:** I can't stand Jane any longer. I want you to fire her today.
**You:** I can't fire Jane today.
**Supervisor:** Oh, yes, you can. She's a disaster.

**You:** I can't fire Jane today.
**Supervisor:** You do what I say or you are in trouble.
**You:** I can't fire Jane today.

Is this skill risky? Perhaps. But isn't it risky if we allow the other person to invade our space, to force us to violate our own ethics or principles?

What the brief, repetitive statement does is convince the other person that we will "hold our ground." About the third time the person hears the statement, he or she stops trying to convince us of his or her need or gets upset and cuts off the conversation. In both cases:

➤ We achieve our goal.
➤ We don't give reasons, accusations, or solutions.
➤ We deliver the message in a non-defensive, non-aggressive, repetitive way.

What requires the most discipline is to not give the other person a solution. The last thing he or she wants to hear is our own solutions to how he or she should behave:

**Example 1:**
"Call the person back later."
"Find a phone of your own."

**Example 2:**
"You don't like Jane. You fire her."
"I think you are wrong to ask me to fire Jane."

We now know the skill: repeat the same line without providing any solution, without justification or defense. We also need to know when to use it: declaration is used only with persistent, stubborn people who are trying to convince us of something.

What is used more often in other situations are the two following skills—straight talk and emotional stand.

## Straight Talk

Straight talk is exactly that.

➤ It identifies the problem.
➤ It states the desired result.
➤ It gives indisputable reasons.

And nothing else! No justifications, no solutions, no nagging, no criticisms. As Jack Webb used to say on *Dragnet*, the old police TV series, "Just the facts, nothing else, just the facts."

Here's a demonstration of straight talk applied to one of the examples given above:

| *Problem* | + | *Behavior* |
|---|---|---|
| I need the phone | | because I'm expecting a scheduled phone call. |

Another major difference between a *declaration* and *straight talk* is that we use straight talk in conjunction with Responsible Listening. We prove we heard the person each time, then repeat our straight talk again.

*Example:*

*Straight Talk:* I need the phone now because I'm expecting a scheduled phone call.
**Other Person:** I'll be off the phone in a minute.
*Listening*: I know you say you'll be off the phone in a minute.
*Straight Talk*: But I need the phone now because I'm expecting a scheduled phone call.
**Other Person:** I'm almost finished with my conversation.
*Listening:* You may almost be finished
*Straight Talk:* But I need the phone now because I'm expecting a scheduled phone call.

### Biggest Mistake When Using Straight Talk

The biggest mistake we can make in using straight talk is to switch from *what we need* to telling the other person *what to do (solution)* and/or *what's wrong with him or her (judgment)*.

For example, instead of saying, "I need the phone now because I'm expecting a phone call," we let our anger and frustration get the best of us:

➤ I need the phone now because "you" can use your own phone (solution).
➤ I need the phone now because "you" can find another phone (solution).
➤ I need the phone now because "you" are being inconsiderate of my time (judgment).
➤ I need the phone now because "you" are causing me a problem (judgment).

Straight talk works only when we describe *our need* in terms of the *effect on us* ("because I'm expecting a scheduled phone call"). The moment we switch from an "I" message to a "You" message ("because you can find another phone"), the other person will get defensive and rightly so, since we are telling them what to do.

Here's an opportunity to practice straight talk with the situations you listed earlier. Formulate a straight talk message for each situation.

*Example:*   State behavior          +          Give reasons for need

*Example:* I need my phone                    because I'm expecting
         now                                  a scheduled phone call
         I can't fire Jane today              because I do not have
                                   the facts

            *Behavior*                    *Reasons for Need*

1.

2.

3.

Straight talk, combined with Responsible Listening, is used in business situations more often than declarations or emotional stands. Most people will respond to our repeated, firm statement of what we need and why we need it.

Sometimes they do not hear us because their own needs may outweigh their ability to listen and respond. When we have tried straight talk, we may have to move to our last resort, an emotional stand.

## Emotional Stand

When we have tried straight talk and it hasn't worked, we need to draw a final line in the sand. We need to add how we feel about what is happening.

Here's the example of all three skills given earlier:

**Declaration:** "I need the phone now." (our need)
**Straight Talk:** "I need the phone now (our need) because I'm expecting a scheduled phone call. (effect on us because of the other person's behavior—not a description of the behavior)
**Emotional Stand:** "When you are talking on my phone and I can't get a scheduled phone call, I get mad because I can't keep my commitment to the other person."

This third skill is called an emotional stand because we state clearly how we feel about the behavior—I'm mad, I'm sad, I'm disappointed, I'm frustrated. We state our feeling with *full intensity, including nonverbals.* For example, if you say, "I'm mad," you might reinforce that verbal message with a red face, an impatient tone, a finger pointing at your chest, your arms outstretched.

The emotional stand works because we are taking a stand for ourselves. We are not stating anything that is debatable: "when you are talking on my phone" (not debatable, but a fact), "I get mad" (my feeling—not debatable), "because I can't keep my commitment to the other person" (not debatable, but a fact). Of course, the other person might tell you that you shouldn't get mad. But nobody can deny that you are, in fact, feeling mad. That's a fact.

The secret to the emotional stand is that everything described is a fact about me. I never attack the character or the motivations of the other person ("you" messages).

Here's an opportunity to practice the emotional stand, at least in written form. List below, under the example, three of your own situations that, if you had a chance to do over again, you might handle with the three-part emotional stand:

| 1. Behavior ("When you …") | 2. Feeling ("I get …") | 3. Effect ("because …") |
|---|---|---|

*Example:*

| When you're talking on my phone | I get mad | because I can't keep my commitment to the other person. |
|---|---|---|

1.

2.

3.

## Summary

Three skills of Declaring are used infrequently in business because most conversations involve mutual problem solving. If we are skilled at Responsible Speaking and Responsible Listening, we can reach our goals. However, without the three skills of Declaring, we might be forced in difficult conversations to make a choice between two ineffective methods—either lose our temper and attack or go quiet and withdraw, still upset.

Again, here's how a full conversation using all these skills might do:

**Me:** I need the phone now. (declarative statement)
**Other:** I'll be done in a minute.
**Me:** I need the phone now because I'm expecting a scheduled phone call. (straight talk)
**Other:** I'm almost finished with the call!
**Me:** When you are talking on my phone and I can't get a scheduled phone call, I get mad because I can't keep my commitment to the other person. (emotional stand)

Declaring is an essential communication skill. Of all the skills, it needs to be short, precise, and patient. We are taking an ethical stand for ourselves. If we believe the situation warrants it, Declaring is the skill to use.

CHAPTER *11*

# Master High-Impact Communications Skills: Your Career and Your Life Depend on It

*T*his final chapter is a request that you master high-impact communication skills. Your career and your life depend on it!

We communicate 90% of our waking hours—and few of us spend any time each day studying what we do during that 90%.

Here's the last coaching story. It is the one that I will never forget. It is the one in which a talented executive saved her career in the first 30 minutes of our first coaching session.

---

### Eliminating a Stutter Put Me Back on the Fast Track

We unconsciously bring to our workplace communication habits we learned in school, habits that have long-term effects on our career. One example is of an executive who stuttered.

Our first coaching session went like this:

**Pete:** Why do you stutter?

---

**Client:** I had poor grades in communications and my teachers urged me to speak up; they made me make spontaneous speeches.

**Pete:** When do you stutter?

**Client:** I think I stutter when I'm unsure of things I'm talking about.

**Pete:** Do you mean to tell me the only time you stutter is when you talk about things you're not sure of?

**Client:** I think so.

**Pete:** Never do that again! Never respond to any questions about something you're unsure of! We will work on helping you to ask questions for clarification, to help you narrow the question to something you know something about. If you can't do that, indicate you don't have the information now but you'll get the answer for them.

She quickly related to that. Miraculously, from that moment on, she didn't stutter! She just never allowed herself to be placed in the position of responding to something of which she was unsure!

## All Communications Are Learned Behaviors and Can Be Relearned

This executive had learned how to stutter. All our communication habits are learned behaviors. Therefore, they can be relearned. Most of the new learning takes place when we become aware of what we don't know. This executive did not know why she stuttered. Once she knew, skill training helped her break the habit.

The rest of this last chapter provides quotes from highly motivated executives who have modified or retrained their communication. They decided *to be their own executive coaches*! Here's what they had to say:

➤ Becoming a better listener has made me a better manager. The feedback that my customers have given me is that I am much more supportive and understanding of their needs since I made the change. And when they're happy, I'm happy!

➤ I used to always fill the silence at a meeting. By listening better and speaking less, my meetings are shorter and projects are more clearly understood. We accomplish more. I work better with my staff, with business partners, and with my bosses. The pressures are still there, but I now have tools to help us find the best solutions.

➤ The "unequal conversation" concept was a powerful eye-opener. It has saved me many hours and probably many relationships by recognizing that when emotions are out, effective communication stops. In just a few months, it has made us more productive by defusing emotion and focusing on the business issues. The only "problem" with embracing these new skills is that, afterwards, you'll wish everyone else did too!

➤ Recognizing communication deficiencies is only half the battle. One also needs the proper tools with which to improve the process. After years of blind attempts at improvement, Responsible Communications provided the road map.

➤ When you are having a conversation with yourself, you are driving yourself crazy. When you are truly listening to another in the conversation, you are finding solutions.

➤ Peter's methods taught me to slow down and really listen to what was being said. His Responsible Listening drills helped me assume responsibility for all my communications.

➤ It is not what you say but instead how you say it.

➤ Before I left your office on our last coaching session, I promised to get back to you on what I found to be the most important things I gained from my training with you. Now, several months later, I find what is consistently the most useful thing to remember and practice is your adage: *every conversation is a sales call.*

Although it requires an effort not to slip back to being a timid communicator, I feel a transformation when I remember your adage. I want to admit that I do slip when I go back to my family. This has frankly been discouraging. And I'm sure it is no coincidence that I am most inclined to slip also when

I am back at my 'family' in the office. It is really hard to break old patterns within old established relationships. But even here, I am making progress.

Another skill you taught is how to effectively confront someone. For me, it takes discipline to think through and plan my approach when I feel offended. Instead, my knee-jerk reaction would be ineffective fighting. But the end result is phenomenally more successful when I implement your approach.

A weak point for me still is listening—I honestly do not practice the skill you taught about listening for a word or idea and using this in my reply.

I also struggled with not telling every single minutia to make a point or answer a question. I cringe when I listen to the tapes from our sessions and I hear myself droning on and on. Speaking of droning ... I guess I should sum this up.

➤ When you first used the term "I am 100% responsible for understanding what other people are saying," I was confused and refused to accept the concept. After you repeated, restated, and explained the concept, I finally made the connection. As I expressed to you, I felt a great sense of relief and release. No longer would I need to feel in control and responsible for those I am communicating with.

➤ I mentioned trying to resolve conflict within my staff and how difficult I found that to be. I was in a stressful situation with staff members who could not get along; I was constantly in the middle, getting them together, reviewing the issues, and trying to mediate them. I now have an entirely new idea of my role in these situations and feel a burden has been lifted from my shoulders.

➤ There is no question about the power to be gained from mastering the communication skills you provide. When I take the time to prepare, I know I will go into a situation with a greater likelihood of success. The biggest challenges are taking the time each day to review the key skills and making the time to prepare for key communication events.

➤ The single most important lesson was to take responsibility for all communications. There are still times when I regress and label another person rather than accept a failure as my own. Regardless, I know in hindsight, I did not do all I could if the communication was ineffective.

➤ On behalf of my family and my company, thank you for sharing your knowledge and experience with me. I am a far richer person because of your tutelage.

## The End of the Beginning

My end is to thank all the executives I have been privileged to coach who made this book possible. This book is their book. It is about how they began to be their own executive coach.

I hope through their experiences you are now motivated to

Master High-Impact Communications Skills For

➤ dealing with difficult people
➤ improving your personal image
➤ learning how to listen
➤ solving business problems creatively

When you do, you will have accomplished a courageous, death-defying act that will help keep your career ... and your life ... on the fast track.

## APPENDIX

# Resources

Thomas H. Gordon, *Leader Effectiveness Training: L.E.T.: The Foundation for Participative Management and Employee Involvement* (New York: Putnam, 1997).

Thomas H. Gordon, *P.E.T.: Parent Effectiveness Training* (New York: New American Library, 1990).

Marvin T. Brown, *Working Ethics: Strategies for Decision Making and Organizational Responsibility* (San Francisco: Jossey-Bass, 1990).

David Michael Levin, *The Listening Self: Personal Growth, Social Change and the Closure of Metaphysics* (New York: Routledge, 1989).

Robert Bolton, *People Skills* (New York: Touchstone Book by Simon and Schuster, 1996).

John Robert Stewart, editor, *Bridges, Not Walls: A Book About Interpersonal Communication* (New York: McGraw-Hill, 1998)

Peter M. Senge, *The Fifth Discipline: The Art and Science of the Learning Organization* (New York: Doubleday Currency, 1991).

Charles H. Kraft, *Communication Theory for Christian Witness* (Maryknoll, NY: Orbis Books, 1991).

Jon R. Katzenbach and Douglas K. Smith, *The Wisdom of Teams: Creating the High-Performance Organization* (New York: Harper Business, 1993).

Stephen R. Covey, *The Seven Habits of Highly Effective People: Powerful Lessons in Personal Change* (New York: Simon and Schuster, 1989).

Daniel Goleman, *Emotional Intelligence: Why It Can Matter More Than IQ for Character, Health and Lifelong Achievement* (New York: Bantam Books, 1995).

Bryan W. Mattimore, *99% Inspiration: Tips, Tales & Techniques for Liberating Your Business Creativity* (New York: AMACOM, 1993).

Daniel Goleman, "What Makes a Leader?" *Harvard Business Review*, November-December 1998.

Philip Yancey, *The Jesus I Never Knew* (Grand Rapids, MI: Zondervan Publishing House, 1995).

## Articles by Peter deLisser:

"Give the Gift of Listening," *International Listening Association Newsletter*, 57 (summer 1996).

"My Boss Is a Screamer," *AICPA The Financial Managers Report*, November 1993.

"Every Conversation Is a Sales Call," *Lamplighter*, vol. 37, American Society for Training and Development, New York Metro Chapter.

"The Quality of Life Depends on the Quality of Communications," unpublished.

"Are We Credible?" unpublished.

"Change Your Communications, Change Your Life," unpublished.

"Human Communication Process," unpublished.

"What Is the Agenda for This Meeting?" *Lamplighter*, vol. 37, American Society for Training and Development, New York Metro Chapter.

"Master High-Impact Communications Skills: Tips to Fast-Track Your Career," *Rockland Business Advocate*, Rockland (NY) Business Association.

# INDEX

## A

action plans
    for responsible listening, 77–79
    for responsible speaking, 106,
        107–109, 108
admiration, rationalizing, 66
aggression, tempering, 62. *See also*
    anger; conflict
agreement
    as basic part of conversations, 6, 47
    defined, 101
    securing, 95, 96, 104–106
anger
    rationalizing, 65, 71–74
    and straight talk, 129
    and structuring conversations, 50
    *See also* conflict; emotions
attention
    as basic part of conversations, 6, 47
    capturing, 94, 95, 97–99
    authority, dealing effectively with,
        14–15, 17, 71–74
awareness, 118
    of communication roadblocks,
        22–31

of conversation quality, 20–22
of personal beliefs, 18–20
of personal experiences, 14–18
of strengths, 10–14

## B

beliefs, 18–20
benefits
    as basic part of conversations, 6, 47
    examples of, 99
    explaining, 99–104
    overview of, 90

## C

clarifying statements, 128
Coaching
    defined, 119
    overview of, 120–22
    versus players and critics, 123–24
    practice drill for, 129
    skills for, 126–28
    when appropriate, 124–25
comfort motivations, 104
commitment
    securing, 99, 100
    to team members, 53